*f*ive Practices
of Fruitful Living

Robert Schnase

Abingdon Press
Nashville

FIVE PRACTICES
OF FRUITFUL LIVING

This book is printed on acid-free paper.

Library of Congress Cataloging-in-Publication Data

Schnase, Robert C.
  Five practices of fruitful living / by Robert Schnase.
    p. cm.
  ISBN 978-1-4267-0880-0 (alk. paper)
  1. Christian life—Methodist authors. I. Title.
  BV4501.3.S354 2010
  248.4'87—dc22
                         2009050661

10 11 12 13 14 15 16 17 18 19—10 9 8 7 6 5 4 3 2 1

MANUFACTURED IN THE UNITED STATES OF AMERICA

Contents

Acknowledgments

Working on this project has been a gift. I've been granted the privilege of exploring the spiritual life more personally and thoughtfully and of rediscovering the grace of friendship. This book is the fruit of many conversations with colleagues, pastors, and lay members. I am indebted to far more people than I could possibly name.

My thanks to the many friends and mentors who have encouraged me. Especially, I appreciate the suggestions and support offered by Janice Huie, Gil Rendle, Ken Carter, Mimi Raper, and Lovett Weems. Judy Davidson has again demonstrated patience and persistence in strengthening my writing. Susan Salley and her team from Abingdon Press have outdone themselves with their guidance and assistance and have helped me tie up many loose ends. I am thankful to Erin Barham and Marcia C'deBaca for the cover design. The support of Dala Dunn and Dick Curry has made my work on this possible. And I offer my personal appreciation to Esther, Karl, and Paul for tolerating the late night tapping on the keyboard during the last many months, and for their willingness to support me in a project that has distracted me from many other important things.

Finally, I give God thanks for the pastors, lay members, and congregations of the Missouri Conference of The United Methodist Church for the joy and privilege of serving with them in Christ's ministry. May our work together be fruitful and to the glory of God.

—Robert Schnase

Introduction

Jesus taught a way of life and invited people into a relationship with God that was vibrant, dynamic, and fruitful. He said, "I am the vine, you are the branches. Those who abide in me and I in them bear much fruit. . . . My father is glorified by this, that you bear much fruit and become my disciples" (John 15:5, 8). Jesus wanted people to flourish.

Scripture is sprinkled with phrases that point to fruitful living—the kingdom of God, eternal life, immeasurable riches, a peace that passes all understanding, abundant life.

Jesus and his followers developed core fundamental spiritual practices that sustained them in God and motivated them to relieve the burdens that restrain people from flourishing by protecting the vulnerable, embracing outcasts, healing the sick, welcoming children, caring for widows, confronting injustice, pardoning sin, preaching good news, releasing people from paralysis and suffering and the fear of death. They presented the gift and demand of God's grace to everyone. They granted peace.

Paul writes, "Let the same mind be in you that was in Christ Jesus" (Philippians 2:5). Scripture is unified around the theme of a vibrant, fruitful, dynamic life with God through following Christ.

How do I have that mind in me that was in Christ? How do I cultivate a life that is abundant, fruitful, purposeful, and deep? What are the commitments, critical risks, and practices that open me to God's transforming grace, and that help me discover the difference God intends for me to make in the world? How do I live the fruitful, flourishing life of a follower of Christ?

Radical Hospitality. Passionate Worship. Intentional Faith Development. Risk-Taking Mission and Service. Extravagant Generosity.

Since the publication of *Five Practices of Fruitful Congregations* (Abingdon Press, 2007), these edgy, provocative, dangerous words have helped hundreds of congregations understand their mission, renew ministries, and stretch toward fruitfulness and excellence for the purposes of Christ.

Five Practices of Fruitful Living moves the discussion of Christian practice from the congregational level to the personal practices of discipleship. The fruitful, God-related life develops with intentional and repeated attention to five essential practices that are critical for our growth in Christ.

Radical Hospitality in our personal walk with Christ begins with an extraordinary receptivity to the grace of God. In distinctive and personal ways, we invite God into our hearts and make space for God in our lives. We receive God's love and offer it to others.

Through the practice of *Passionate Worship*, we learn to love God in return. We practice listening to God, allowing God to shape our hearts and minds through prayer, personal devotion, and community worship. We love God.

Through the practice of *Intentional Faith Development*, we do the soul work that connects us to others, immerses us in God's Word, and positions us to grow in grace and mature in Christ. We learn in community.

The practice of *Risk-Taking Mission and Service* involves offering ourselves in purposeful service to others in need, making a positive difference even at significant personal cost and inconvenience to our own lives. We serve.

Through the practice of *Extravagant Generosity*, we offer our material resources in a manner that supports the causes that transform life and relieve suffering and that enlarges the soul and sustains the spirit. We give back.

These Five Practices—to receive God's love, to love God in return, to grow in Christ, to serve others, and to give back—are so essential to growth in Christ and to the deepening of the spiritual life that failure to attend to them, develop them, and deepen them with intentionality limits our capacity to live fruitfully and fully, to settle ourselves completely in God, and to become instruments of God's transforming grace. The adjectives—*radical, passionate, intentional, risk-taking,* and *extravagant*—provoke us out of complacency and remind us that these practices require more than haphazard, infrequent, and mediocre attention.

These practices open our heart—to God, to others, to a life that matters, a life rich with meaning, relationship, and contribution. They help us flourish.

Christian Practice

The ministry of Jesus is grounded in personal practices. Jesus' life is marked by prayer, solitude, worship, reflection, the study of Scripture, conversation, community, serving, engagement with suffering, and generosity. These personal practices sustained a ministry that opened people to God's grace, transformed human hearts, and changed the circumstances of people in need. Jesus modeled going away to quiet places, spending time in the Temple, and listening for God. Jesus spoke to the woman at the well; the tax collector in the tree; the rich young ruler on the road; the paralyzed man beside the pool; to the lepers and the blind and the widowed and the wealthy; to Mary and Martha and Peter and John. He held a child in his arms, noticed the woman who touched his robe, healed a soldier's servant, ate with sinners, told stories to Pharisees, and blessed the thief beside him on the cross. He intervened to challenge unjust systems that abused vulnerable people, overturning the money changers' tables and dispersing those ready to kill a woman accused of adultery. He connected people to God, opened their hearts and minds to God's kingdom, invited them to follow in his steps, and set them on a path toward God. Jesus knitted them into community, interlaced their lives with one another by the Holy Spirit, and wove them into the body of Christ, the church. By example and story, by lessons and parables, and by inviting them into ministry and sending them out in his name, he taught them to practice and live the ways of God. Jesus made maturing in faith and growth toward God unexpectedly and irresistibly appealing.

This book is based on the premise that by repeating and deepening certain fundamental practices, we cooperate with God in our own growth in Christ and participate with the Holy Spirit in our own spiritual maturation. The fundamental practices are rooted in Scripture and derived from the clear imperatives of the life of Christ; they are distilled through the monastic formative exercises of the early church and are sharpened by the community disciplines of the early Methodists and other renewal movements. They find expression today in congregations throughout the world that intentionally cultivate authentic life in Christ and the formation of Christian character and service.

Picture the graceful performance of a gymnast. With effortless elegance, she balances on the high beam, lifting herself up on a single tiptoe and down again, bows low with arms gracefully outstretched. Her ease of movement, naturalness of posture, and energetic responses make her look entirely at home balancing on a beam only a few inches wide. She bends and stretches in ways that defy ordinary human athleticism, occasionally suspending herself steadily on one hand or two, other times leaping high above the beam as if free of gravity itself. She smiles, breathing easily and smoothly, as if the workout has barely challenged her.

How does she make it look so natural? It looks so easy precisely because she has worked so hard. She has repeated and practiced and rehearsed the hundreds of small incremental motions for years that combine to make possible such ease of movement. What seemed at first to be impossible, or extraordinarily difficult, became progressively easier and more satisfying through months and years of practice. It was not easy or natural until, through repetition, the muscles themselves developed the memory that the art requires. Hundreds of hours of effort, commitment, and practice prepared her to perform so naturally and gracefully.

Or watch young Little League baseball players practice. They scoop up ground balls, catch pop-up flies, throw the ball around the bases, and practice batting.

Now watch professional baseball players practice before a Major League game. These players are paid handsomely; they are elite athletes at the height of their careers. What do they do to practice before each Major League game? They scoop up grounders, catch pop-ups, throw the ball around the bases, and practice batting.

Baseball involves certain fundamental activities, and every play of every game involves those basic elements performed with endless variations. A player simply keeps repeating and improving on the same basic elements. No professional baseball player says, "I don't practice batting anymore because I learned that in high school."

Christian practices are those essential activities we repeat and deepen over time. They create openings for God's Spirit to shape us. They are not steps that we complete and put behind us never to repeat again. And practices are not static qualities that some people naturally possess and others absolutely lack. Anyone can start at any point and at any level and begin to develop the practices; with the help of the Holy Spirit, the practices will change who they are. Practices are not simply principles we talk about; practices are something we do.

Through practices we become "doers of the word, and not merely hearers" (James 1:22), and we weave together faith and action, theology and life, thinking and doing, intention and realization, heart and head with hands. Practices make our faith a tangible and visible part of daily life. We see them done in the life of Jesus, and we do them until they become a way of life for us. Even when we cannot articulate the content of our faith with confidence or detail, through our practice we embody faith and express our ultimate commitment to God and our desire to follow Christ. Practices represent our positive contribution to the transformation of all things through Christ.

Through practice, we open ourselves to grace and let ourselves be opened by grace. We follow Christ, step by step, day by day, again and again; and by these steps and through these days, we are changed, we become someone different, we become new creations in Christ.

This isn't a self-improvement, pull-yourself-up-by-your-own-bootstraps notion of how we grow in grace. It's not about trying harder, working longer, or striving more to achieve God's blessing.

The Christian life is a gift of God, an expression of God's grace in Christ, the result of an undeserved and unmerited offering of love toward us. Every step of the journey toward Christ is preceded by, made possible by, and sustained by the perfecting grace of God.

However, becoming the person that God desires us to become is also the fruit of a persistent and deeply personal quest, an active desire to love God, to allow God's love to lead us. The fruitful life is cultivated by placing ourselves in the most advantageous places to see, receive, learn, and understand the love that has been offered in Christ.

So deeply is the notion of Christian practices embedded in our faith tradition that the name of the Book of Acts in the original Greek is *praxeis*, from which we derive our word *practice*. In the second chapter of the Acts (practices!) of the Apostles, Luke reminds us that the essential activities of Christian living include worshipping God, learning God's Word, serving one another, and sharing generously. The repeated pattern of these practices formed the early Christian church into a community that was so appealing in its purpose and its conduct of life together, that people were added to their number day by day.

The patristic and monastic teachers of the early church developed rich disciplines of daily practice that included hospitality and receptivity; worship and prayer; study and learning in community; service to the ill, poor, and imprisoned; and the stewardship of all earthly possessions. Daily and consistent practice helped Christ's followers accomplish the tasks given by God for the fruitful life. "Christian formation" describes the way our intentionally repeated activities help us cooperate with the Holy Spirit in God's "forming" of us into new creatures.

The early Methodist movement thrived under the rubrics of personal practices—worship, singing, fasting, and receiving the sacraments; searching Scripture and participating in classes and covenant groups for spiritual encouragement and accountability; serving the poor and visiting the sick and imprisoned; and tithing their incomes. John Wesley's was a theology of *grace*, focused on God's initiating love in Christ. The Methodist renewal, however, rested on *practices*, emphasizing the role we play in our own spiritual growth and the perfecting role of community to shape us. Early Wesleyans were chided as "Methodists" because of their nearly eccentric adherence to methodical ways of systemizing the practices of the Christian faith to promote learning, service, and growth in Christ through daily and weekly exercises and patterns.

How to Use This Book

This book is deeply personal, and as such it is composed of stories—the experiences, hopes, doubts, good efforts, and false starts of people like you and me. Faith journeys are used to illustrate key points so as to encourage honest reflection and conversation. But the approach is not individualistic—only about me, my, and mine. Every experience embeds us more deeply in the community of Christ because it is in the presence of our sisters and brothers that our spirits are sustained, our hearts encouraged.

Henri Nouwen believed that what is personal is most universal. When we think we may be the only person who has ever felt a certain way, doubted or feared or resisted in a certain manner, we discover that such experience is usually what we have most in common with others in their innermost lives. Listen to the stories of others in this text. In other people, we find glimpses of ourselves; in their shortfalls, we see our own more clearly; in their callings, we find clues to our own.

Approach this conversation with honesty and openness. Years ago I was pressured by friends to attend a men's weekend retreat. I had better things to do, but I went reluctantly anyway. During prayer on the first evening, one of the leaders said, "Lord, we pray for the person present who needs this retreat the most. And we especially pray for the person present who thinks he needs this retreat the least." I felt as if a spotlight had suddenly shone on me among all the people in the chapel. I realized that I needed to set aside my arrogance and resistance. I unfolded my arms, unclenched my fists, and lifted my eyes to what was before me. I needed to listen. And learn. I needed to open myself to what God's Spirit might reveal to me. With a change of my internal attitude, the retreat became rich, sustaining, and life-changing.

I pray for those who reach for this book searching for understanding about their own faith journeys, that it may stimulate them to a deeper life in Christ. But I pray especially for those who have been handed this book and who open its pages reluctantly, that they may open themselves to the possibility that something in the stories and reflections may cause them to think more deeply, pray more earnestly, and serve others in a more fruitful and satisfying way.

This book is experiential rather than systematic or dogmatic. It relies on the experiences of ordinary people who have been extraordinarily shaped by their relationship to God. None of us has the complete picture. Movement toward Christ is never a straight line, uninterrupted, obstacle free, totally consistent, predictable, and easily describable. There are no perfect accounts that capture everything that lies behind and no completely reliable maps that outline the future in one's faith journey. Soul work is hard; and following Christ is messy, challenging, joyous, scary, painful, sustaining, and frustratingly indescribable.

A professor taught me that doctrine is like the sediment of a moving river. It is the accumulation and compounding over time of tradition, experience, history. This book, though, is about the river—alive, moving, dynamic, changing, powerful, irrepressible. It is about the everyday faith of everyday people seeking to listen for God, to love each other, to care for those in need, to embrace the stranger, to live the fruit of the Spirit.

This book is practical. It is about what we do daily and intentionally, and about who we become because of how God uses what we do. It suggests a compass rather than map; a direction helpful for many diverse contexts rather than a specific step-by-step, how-to plan that fits only certain terrain.

Engage the material personally. Discover what you can learn about yourself, your relationship with God, your personal desires and internal resistances in the life of faith.

And read the book with others on the journey to Christ. Use it in house groups, adult Sunday school classes, a weeknight book study, or with your family. Resolve to deepen your own practices of faith. Pray for one another and support one another in Christ.

Encourage church leaders and pastors to use the book in retreats, sermons series, or evening studies. These five focus the essential work that forms disciples; by cultivating these practices in the lives of those reached by the community of faith, the congregation fulfills its mission of making disciples of Jesus Christ for the transformation of the world.

As a pastor and bishop, I've been granted the privilege of witnessing people whose faith is immeasurably greater than my own; whose sacrifice is more than I myself could ever bear; whose impact in the lives of others through their service is so much greater than mine; whose personal discipline, depth of spirit, and maturing in Christ is far ahead of anything I shall ever achieve or hope to receive; and whose generosity is so extraordinary that it humbles me completely. This book is about how we learn from their fruitfulness in Christ so that we cooperate with God in becoming what God created us to be.

My prayer for you and your congregation is that *Five Practices of Fruitful Living* helps us all grow in grace and in the knowledge and love of God. May we be changed from the inside out so that we can transform the world for the purposes of Christ.

CHAPTER ONE

Receiving God's Love

The Practice of Radical Hospitality

"We love because he first loved us." —1 John 4:19

"Accept that you are accepted." When I read this as a college student, those words by Paul Tillich jolted me into a new understanding of God's unconditional love.[1] The pivotal first element in our walk of faith—the practice of Radical Hospitality—involves our saying *Yes* to God's love for us, a willingness to open our lives to God and invite God into our hearts. It involves our capacity to receive grace, accept Christ's love, and make room for God in our lives.

"Do we know what it means to be struck by grace?" Tillich asks. This was a provocative notion to me, an odd metaphor, to describe God's grace as something that strikes, that jars us into a new way of thinking, that collides with our old way of being. He continues, "We cannot transform our lives, unless we allow them to be transformed by that stroke of grace." The first movement toward the new creation, the transformed life, and becoming the person God wants us to be begins when we face the startling reality of God's unconditional love for us. Receiving the love and forgiveness of God, beginning to comprehend its meaning, and opening ourselves to the new life it brings can be as disrupting as an earthquake, as abrupt as lightening striking across the black night sky. It means we've been struck by grace.

The personal practice of Radical Hospitality begins with a receiving, perceiving, listening, opening, accepting attitude—a readiness to accept and welcome God's initiative toward us. It is sustained with active behaviors that place us in the most advantageous posture to continue to receive God, welcome Christ, and make room for grace. And so it involves interior decision and soul work, a listening and receptivity to God, as well as habits that transform us as we regularly, frequently, and intentionally make room in our lives for God.

Grace strikes at unexpected times, Tillich suggests: when we are in pain, feeling restless, empty, alone, estranged, or when we feel disgust, weakness, or hostility. It strikes us when other things don't work, when we feel directionless and useless, when compulsions reign, and darkness overshadows. When the ordinariness of life grinds us down, or the vacuity of the world's promises leaves us empty, when we finally realize our churning and churning is taking us nowhere fast, in such moments, grace comes to us like a wave of light in the darkness, and we perceive a voice saying, "You are accepted."

"We don't know the name of it at the time; there will be much to learn later," Tillich writes. We don't have to promise anything at the time, for in that moment we are fundamentally the recipients of a promise. We don't have to give anything; only to receive what is given. Our only and singular task is to *accept* that we are accepted.

You are *loved*. You *are* loved. *You* are loved.

Can you accept that?

God's love for us is not something we have to strive for, earn, work on, or fear. It is freely given. That is key: that we are loved, first, finally, and forever by God, a love so deep and profound and significant that God offers his Son to signify and solidify this love forever so that we get it.

The journey to becoming what God would have us to be begins with opening ourselves to this love, and giving it a place in our hearts. The journey begins when the God "up there" or "out there," the God whom we perceive as some philosophical abstraction, becomes a living truth and a love that we receive into ourselves. The welcoming requires of us an extraordinary hospitality, a radical receptivity, a willingness to allow God to come in and dwell within our hearts.

I first read Tillich's essay while sitting on grass near a fountain outside a campus library on a bright spring morning. I'd been active in church for years and was contemplating the call to ministry. I was rethinking the faith of my childhood and struggling with the normal things college students wrestle with. I was more clear about what I did not believe than about what I did believe. A student group at church was reading Tillich, a well-known theologian, and I was doing my assignment.

Tillich describes those things that separate us from God and one another. He writes about feeling unaccepted and about striving to prove, earn, justify, or validate ourselves. This resonated deeply with the feelings of uncertainty, pain, and struggle that I experienced as a student wrestling with the expectations of parents, the pressure of peers, the yearning to fit in, the desire to make a difference. His words somehow stimulated a rush of thoughts about life's meaning, connection, and direction. I kept looking up from the text to the fountain, lost in my own thoughts, yet soothed by whispers of flowing water. The Spirit was breaking through, stirring my soul, and moving me to deeper places.

Accept that you are accepted. In the moment that grace strikes, grace conquers sin. Lingering guilt that has grown tumor-like for years in the dark recesses of a person's soul can lose its deathly power. Grace helps us face the truth about ourselves, to embrace it rather than run from it; and by embracing this truth and offering it to God, we discover that God knows the truth about us and still loves us, and that God will shape us from this day forward anew. God's been waiting for us, desiring us to let him in. Can we accept that we are accepted?

Grace, when we really absorb its full meaning and consequence, causes us to rethink the direction and momentum of our lives, to change course, to break through the pretense and pride and see

Just Say Yes!

Richard wanted to know what we are supposed to say *Yes* to when he first saw the tagline "Say *Yes!*" on all the bulletins, banners, and websites of First United Methodist Church of Sedalia, Missouri. As he began to explore the spiritual life through worship, prayer, Bible study, and service, he realized that every single step in following Christ involves saying *Yes* . . . yes to God, yes to the spiritual life, yes to serving, yes to giving, yes to life.

At what points have you said *Yes* to God when you could have said *No*, and saying *Yes* has made all the difference?

ourselves as we really are—utterly and completely unable by our own striving and effort to make it all work. The love of God pierces the veneer, breaks through the resistances, pulls us out of ourselves, and takes us into the deepest of mysteries of the spiritual life. Our worth is grounded in God's grace. When we finally get it, and open our hearts to the truth of God's love for us, we begin to receive glimpses of a peace that the world cannot give or take away, an inner assurance about our ultimate worth in God's eyes that surpasses understanding.

God creates us. God loves us. God desires a relationship with us.

In the revealing moment, our singular task is not to harden our hearts but to open them to God, to open our lives to grace, to receive, and to say *Yes*. Radical Hospitality begins by welcoming God in rather than slamming the door closed.

Have you ever been struck by grace?

Reading those words by Tillich more than thirty years ago, I could see so many of the events of my faith journey with greater clarity, the initiative of God's grace reaching out to me through the lives of many people. God has wanted in.

I experienced the feeling of life beginning anew, taking hold. In that moment, the rest of my life was given to me as a gift.

Accept that you are accepted. Open the doors of your heart.

A Look at Grace

Can you remember one moment in your life that changed all the others? Have you experienced an event that caused the ground to shift beneath you? Have you ever experienced the unexpected and irreversible unraveling of all the previous understandings of yourself and your world? What has been the most overwhelming and determining experience of your life? A love? A loss? A birth? A truth?

Accepting that you are accepted can be such a moment. Being struck by grace can prove such a time. Inviting God in alters everything. Love changes us, and through us, it changes others around us.

Scripture tells many stories of unexpected grace. Saul on the Damascus road, Zacchaeus, Mary Magdalene, the woman beside the well, the worshipful Mary and her obsessive sister Martha, the man paralyzed beside the pool, the woman accused of adultery, the soldier with a dying servant, the thief on the cross—what happened to them all? Struck by grace each and every one, penetrated by the unfathomable and overwhelming truth of God's love for them, their self-images shattered and replaced with a whole new way of seeing themselves and the world, their old ways broken by an amazing grace. In both ordinary and radical ways, they opened their hearts to God and invited God in.

Through Jesus, God said *Yes* to them, and each in her or his own way found the courage to say *Yes* to God; and in that interchange, all things became new. God's welcoming of them was met with a new hospitality toward God.

The Mystery of Grace

"I do not at all understand the mystery of grace—only that it meets us where we are but does not leave us where it found us."[2]
—Anne Lamott

God's love has a piercing quality, a persevering element, an assertive and searching aspect. God yearns for us, woos us, reaches for us. God's grace has the generative power to pardon, transform, redeem, and perfect, and it pushes and pursues. God's love is not something sitting on a shelf that we reach for, but a truth at the heart of life that reaches for us. God's grace interrupts with a compelling, propelling, motivating, and mobilizing quality. It has the power, if we let it, to break open our hearts, get inside of us, change us, and then work its way through us to others.

The experience and insight of countless of our forebears for hundreds of years is that when we delve deeply into the interior life and begin the spiritual journey, we seek what is true and good only to discover that something is seeking us; that in our yearning, something longs for us; in our desire to know, we find ourselves known. It's not that we love first, but that we are first loved. This active, reaching quality of God's love is what *grace* refers to, a gift-like initiative on God's part toward us. On the

Sistine Chapel ceiling, Michelangelo's famous painting depicts humanity reaching for God only to discover God reaching all the more toward us.

God loves you. Period.

And the first critical step in the journey of faith involves a Radical Hospitality, our opening our hearts to God's love, letting God into our lives to work with us.

Every person we admire, respect, and desire to emulate for their spirituality, wisdom, graciousness, service, and generosity at some point explicitly and dramatically, or unknowingly and gradually, decided to let God in. They said *Yes* to God's love, and opened the door to allow God in. They didn't have all their beliefs figured out, and maybe they still don't, but in their pattern of receiving, God stopped being merely an idea and became personal for them, a part of them, an element of their daily lives, a resident in their heart. They accepted God's acceptance of them, and allowed this truth to shape and change them, dramatically and quickly in some and gradually in others.

Paul writes, "For by *grace* you have been *saved* through *faith*, and this is not your own doing; it is the gift of God" (Ephesians 2:8, emphasis added). *Saved* means that we come into a right relationship with God, becoming what God created us to be. *Saved* refers to our becoming whole, our living fully and abundantly the fruitful life. Paul says there are two essential and operative elements to this whole and right relationship with God, *grace* and *faith*.

Grace refers to the gift-like quality of God's love, the initiating power and presence of God in our lives. *Grace* is God accepting us, despite our rejecting or ignoring or rebelling against God's love. *Grace* is God offering us a relationship, loving us. It is the unexpected UPS package delivered to our front door with our name on it.

Faith is our acceptance of the gift, the opening of our hearts to invite God's love into our lives. *Faith* is our receiving God's grace, love, and pardon, and allowing these gifts to shape us and make us anew. *Faith* is the commitment again and again to live by grace, to honor the gift, and use it, and pass it along. *Faith* is accepting the UPS package, signing on the dotted line, taking it inside our house, unwrapping it, and discovering its treasure.

God's gracious love for us, and the capacity for that love to change our lives when we open ourselves to it, and through us to change the world—this is the central story of the Christian journey. "For God so loved the world that he gave his only Son, so that everyone who believes in him may not perish but may have eternal life" (John 3:16). This verse, the "Gospel in Miniature," captures the interchange between grace and faith and the new life it brings.

Jesus is the ultimate expression of God's grace, God becoming human in order to reach us and to make possible living abundantly, meaningfully, lovingly, and gracefully.

Frequently, we view God as some cosmic entity existing beyond our experience, removed from daily life, an abstraction of the mind. But the God we see revealed in Jesus Christ is not some passive general benevolence that leaves things alone. The God we see revealed in Jesus is the God of *grace*, an active, searching, embracing, assertive love. It is a strong, persevering, gritty grace that gives Jesus the power to embrace untouchable lepers, sit with outcast tax collectors, visit with forbidden strangers. The grace of the Lord Jesus Christ is the steel courage to intercede against the violence and injustice of angry authorities on behalf of a woman accused of adultery. It is an earthy, practical grace that causes Jesus to kneel before his friends, take a towel from his waist and wash their feet, daring them to do likewise as a way of life. It is an unrelenting and irresistible grace that never gives up on either the hopeless and despairing or the rich and powerful. It is the disturbing, interruptive grace that overturns the tables of the cheating money changer in the Temple. It is the perceptive, affirming grace that notices the widow with her two coins, a father anxious about his epileptic son, a farmer pruning vines. It is the compassionate grace that embraces the victims of violence, and the persistent grace that steps into cell blocks with prisoners. It is the challenging, correcting, indicting grace that confronts unjust judges, self-justifying lawyers, unsympathetic rich people, and haughty religious leaders. It is the costly, sacrificial grace that dares to absorb the violence of humiliation, unjust persecution, and torturous death to reveal the depth of God's love for humanity.

The love of God revealed in Jesus extends to the outcast and the insider, the despairing and the self-satisfied, to the religious as well as to those who actively or indifferently reject faith.

Jesus not only loved people no one else loved, but his grace also extended to the unlovable and hidden parts of those who lived otherwise good and faithful lives. By washing the feet of his disciples, Jesus symbolically touched the dirtiest, most offensive part of each person's life, demonstrating an unexpected love. Grace is God's loving activity embracing our lostness, brokenness, hurt, and rebellion, so that we may experience forgiveness, reconciliation, and liberation, which come only through our receiving this love into our lives. A radical encounter with the grace of God may not solve everything overnight, but many things remain beyond our ability to solve until we at least take the first step of accepting the grace of God and inviting God's love in.

The piercing quality of God's love disrupts people. It does not leave us alone and will not let us go. This love breaks through pretense, shatters previous self-understandings, reshapes priorities, turns the world upside down. Being struck by grace is not simply adopting a new attitude, feeling better about ourselves, changing our image, or giving ourselves a lift. The result of Radical Hospitality, a cultivated receptivity to God's grace, causes people who are going down one path to change direction and take another instead.

John Wesley, the founder of Methodism, discovered that even he himself could be unexpectedly struck anew by God's grace. He records in his journal a moment when the reality of God's grace pierced his heart, changing him again forever. "In the evening I went very unwillingly to a society in Aldersgate Street, where one was reading Luther's preface to the Epistle to the Romans. About a quarter before nine, while he was describing the change which God works in the heart through faith in Christ, I felt my heart strangely warmed. I felt I did trust in Christ, in Christ alone for salvation; And an assurance was given me, that he had taken away *my* sins, even *mine*, and saved *me* from the law of sin and death."[3]

Accept that you are accepted. The most important journey you will ever take begins by saying *Yes*, by receiving God's love and accepting God's acceptance of you. With lives filtered through a promise, the followers of Jesus live sustained by the assurance of God's unending love. A continuing receptivity to God's initiative in our lives is the key to all the practices that lead to fruitful living.

God loves you. This is the story of grace. If this is so, why is it so hard for us to hear and know this truth?

Distractions, Defenses, and Complicity

Ten thousand obstacles prevent our receiving God's love and make us inhospitable to God's initiative. We fail to open ourselves to God's love, even when we hear these words spoken to us because other voices are repeated even more frequently.

Cultural Voices

The voices of our commercial culture repeat themselves over and over, influencing us through television, radio, magazines, billboards, the Internet, iPods and iPhones; and all these voices penetrate our lives to influence our perceptions of ourselves. Like a magnet beside a compass that draws the needle away from its true bearing, these cultural voices make it hard for us to move in directions that are positive, that lead to peace and happiness, or that open us to the spiritual life. We have difficulty valuing things appropriately. These influences feed the myth that our worth and happiness rest with what kind of car we drive or clothes we wear, or what kind of "look" we have or income we earn.

An interesting contradiction puzzles sociologists and psychologists. Since World War II, we've faced a time of unprecedented prosperity and material well-being in Western societies. No era in human history has ever been more richly blessed with progress in health, longevity, protection from the elements, speed of transportation and ease of communication, safety from illness and pandemic and famine, and security from the violence of war. We've had more liberty, more choices, more options, more mobility, and more freedom from fear than at any time in the history of the earth.[4]

So, why have we not been happier? Why have nearly all measures of contentedness, connection, and a sustaining sense of purpose declined? As we've developed the practical, technical, and material skills for living prosperously, the spiritual skills for living happily, wisely, generously, and meaningfully have weakened. Cultural voices replay the myth that a good life comes from the practice of buying, possessing, and accumulating, and this fosters a thin, elusive, transient, watery happiness. The thick, rich, lasting notion of a good life, of life abundant and fruitful, comes from deeper sources. It grows from the awareness that God loves us, and from the persistent soul work, the repeated opening of ourselves to God to let ourselves be changed, and from loving and being loved by others. This alone stands as the unassailable and intrinsic source of our living happily, peacefully, and fruitfully.

Fast-Forward Living

The rapid speed and intensity of our high-tech and highly mobile lifestyles distract us from fathoming the spiritual life and the depth of God's love for us. For many of us, every moment of our waking days is filled with movement, activity, and sound. Directed by our hand-held planners and connected by our computers and cell phones, we move in fast-forward from home to work and back again, to children's activities, sports events, entertainment venues, fast food restaurants. From the awakening alarm until the final "click" closing our Internet browsers, our lives are surrounded by sensations that keep us focused on the motion and movement of the physical world, immersed in tangible sounds and sights and the pressing immediacy of what's expected next from us.

The risk is a rather shallow and surface existence, investing enormous amounts of time, passion, and energy in many things that simply do not merit it—distractedly and purposelessly surfing the Net, noodling away time with computer games, flipping channels through an array of admittedly vacuous choices on television.

These are the cultural waters through which we swim daily, and life is too short not to spend some time in pure escape, unapologetically enjoying our leisure.

On the other hand, where does a pattern of twenty or thirty years of unrestrained and unreflective immersion in these distractions and entertainments take us? How do these form us? What kind of person do they help us become? Everything we do is a spiritual practice, building up or tearing down our spiritual fabric, deepening or ignoring life with God. Do our current patterns enrich our spirits and glorify God, or impoverish our inner life and avoid God?

Name one person you desire to model your life after because of what he or she consumes, or because of all the television he or she watches, or celebrity details he or she knows.

It Fits Me Better

Gloria describes the sudden truth that occurred to her one day as she found herself cleaning up the beer cans the morning after a late night of channel surfing with her husband. The number of cans kept growing. "What kind of life is this? Where is this going?" she and her husband asked themselves. They decided to risk something different. They began to explore the spiritual life by attending a congregation. The whole environment was new to them, but they kept opening themselves to new experiences. They discovered others who were also searching. Gradually, they found themselves shifting how they used their time, what they talked about, what activities they connected to. Five years later Gloria says, "We changed in ways we couldn't have imagined. My life as I live it now would be a total stranger to my former self. I'm becoming a different person, and it fits me better."

Intuitively, we know that this type of living does not lead to the rich-textured life that ultimately satisfies. We perceive the difference between living thinly, and living deeply, fruitfully, and abundantly. Life lived entirely on the superficial level lacks depth, purpose, connection. It misses the sacred. It avoids the spiritual, and we are at greater risk of this than we sometimes acknowledge. Distracted by television, the Internet, and iPods and focused on the recurring urgencies of making a living, maintaining our health, paying the bills, fulfilling our basic family obligations—there's hardly time or space to contemplate where all this is taking us. Like water bugs skimming dizzily in circles on the surface of a pool, we can live oblivious to the depth and height and expanse of existence.

Paul warns about this danger when he writes, "Do not be conformed to this world. . . ." (Romans 12:2), or as one translation says, "Don't let the world . . . squeeze you into its own mold" (JBP).

The conscientious person trying to figure out how to flourish amidst the daily influences of the culture perceives an underlying question: How do I find God in this world in which I live? How do I allow God into my life? Those mentors and examples of fruitful living we admire have discovered what Paul calls the "indescribable gift" of God's grace (2 Corinthians 9:15). They have opened themselves more deeply to the interior life, the life of soul and spirit, the path of the holy and sacred. They have made critical choices and developed patterns and practices of living that have helped them access life with God.

God is in the depth, and we lose touch with God when we focus only on surface things. God is in the silence which we neglect and fear, and we close ourselves to the whisperings of the Spirit when we constantly surround ourselves with artificial sounds. God is in the questions that arise when we break free of the distractions, and we cut God off when we avoid contemplations of purpose, value, and priority. God is in the mystery, and we turn God away when we live as if the only things that matter are those we can see, touch, explain, or possess. God is in the love of others, and we drive God out when we neglect the deepening of relationships. God is in the feeling of being still, and we overlook attempts by God to reach us when we run constantly from one activity to another. God is in the discovery and exploration of the interior life, and we say *No* to God when we deny there is a spiritual side to our own lives. There are elements to existence that we only discover when we open ourselves to God.

The fast-forward focus on surface things contrasts with the lives our ancestors lived. Our great-grandparents spent long hours in repetitive tasks, usually with other members of their family or community, working with their hands, surrounded by the natural sounds of home, farm, kitchen, neighborhood, and community. Whether they worked the fields, hunted in the woods, labored in the workshop, or sweated in the kitchen, most had hours each day to think, remember, mull over, rehearse, and reflect on the happenings of their lives. The meaning of events filtered regularly through a thousand internal permutations and reconsiderations, tested and shaped by conversation and community. Their routines gave time for the mind and heart to contemplate and to connect to others.

Today, it's hard to develop the interior capacity to listen for God or the readiness of soul that makes room for God's grace. Distraction dulls us to the sharper truths. We lose something when we are too distracted; having no deep relationships changes us. Like passengers on a speeding train trying to hear the whispers of a stranger standing beside the tracks, the dizzying intensity, unrelenting forward motion, and insulation of our culture make it hard for us to really hear God's word and feel God's love. Hearing God requires deliberate soul work. Spirituality and speed do not go together well.

Fifty or sixty years of a life defined by doing what's next, responding to the expectations of others, shaped entirely by the urgencies of work and the voices of culture—that's the risk of superficial living. If we do not intentionally ask, "What am I here for?" and "Where am I going?" these cultural influences will propel us along the surface of life, forming an identity not of our own shaping and providing a destination not of our own choosing. We can become what we never intended to be.

Unfortunately, even our religious involvements may contribute nothing but additional activity on the surface level of living if those involvements merely support the same values and goals that conform us to the world. Attending programs, meetings, and performances, we may find ourselves behaving outwardly religious while avoiding genuine explorations of the interior life. It's as easy to close the door to God's grace in our church life as it is in our life at home, work, or leisure. We can sing the choruses of how Jesus loves us while inwardly failing to make space in our souls for the truly transforming power of that love. Religion must do more than just help us fit in better and get ahead faster according to the world's values.

Negative Internal Messages

In addition to external distractions, internal pressures also complicate receiving God's love—negative family voices that replay through our minds, distorting our ability to absorb the truth that God loves us. The struggles we've had to overcome in order to feel loved, accepted, respected, or appreciated limit our ability to receive God's love. Many of us still endlessly pursue the affirmation of a father or mother, even if they are deceased, or we strive to win the approval of a significant teacher, coach, or mentor whose disapproving voice we internalized many years ago. This unmet yearning makes it difficult for us to open ourselves to the truth that God's love is not something we have to struggle for.

Part of every childhood involves balancing the signs of parental love and approval with the expressions of disappointment, disapproval, and disinterest that we perceive. Many of us grow up convinced that we are not good enough, smart enough, important enough, athletic enough, or attractive enough to receive the love and affirmation that we need or desire. Love, even from parents, seems to have a conditional edge to it—more present when we acquiesce to the desires they have for us, or when we excel, win, and achieve than when we fail, stumble, struggle, or go our own way. Sometimes parents mete out love and approval in direct proportion to a child's success and achievement, and trying to earn parental love means pursuing an ever-receding goal.

Such unresolved personal issues block our ability to receive true unconditional love from God. We say God loves us as a father loves his own, or that God's grace sustains us as a mother embraces her children, without considering the limitations of these metaphors for people who have experienced neglect, judgment, anger, or distance from parents, or who have struggled unsuccessfully for years to earn affection.

Attitudes, Choices, Behaviors

We create our own obstacles to God's grace. We willfully deny God's gracious offer of love. By our own attitudes and behaviors we resist grace and its implications that would change us, and avoid real engagement with the interior life and its truths. We feed selfishness, self-preoccupation, and self-absorption that separate us from God and others, feverishly nurturing the resentments we harbor toward others that we do not want to let go of.

All of us have a history, and have made enough destructive decisions that create large reservoirs of private shame, guilt, and regret. Desiring to follow Christ, many of us pack as if we misunderstand the purpose of the trip, bringing with us animosities, conflicts, control issues, and insecurities that weigh us down but which we find difficult to leave behind. Insistently hanging on shuts the door to God's grace and stops us from following the way of Christ. Deep envy; unresolved jealousy; inappropriate sexual appetite; self-isolating greed; and poisonous anger, bitterness, or violence—these give us a closed posture toward God, a fear of the talk of grace and of love. We become defensive and resolute in resisting God's grace, running from God, keeping the truth from penetrating us. Clinging to life as we've come to live it, even if it feels unsatisfying or desolate, seems deceptively easier than change.

Jesus tells three stories in the fifteenth chapter of Luke that capture our disconnection from God's searching grace. The first is about Distraction. People are like sheep who distractedly nibble their way lost, mindlessly moving from one green tuft of grass to another until they are somewhere they never intended. The second is about Clutter. Why did the woman have such a difficult time finding the lost coin in her own home? Was her environment so messy, so cluttered, or so crowded that what she valued could no longer be seen without effort? She has to clean and search to rediscover what was lost. The third is about Willful Rebellion. The prodigal son runs away from his father, consciously complicit in his own self-destructive impulses. These stories remind us that the

---

"Me? Asking *God?"*

Joe Eszterhas's successful films won awards and earned him millions. But even with throat cancer destroying his larynx, he could not shake his life-long and life-threatening addictions to alcohol and tobacco. One hot sunny day, trying to outwalk fear, panic, and death, he sat down on the curb, sweating, crying, hyperventilating. He listened to himself moaning, and he heard himself mumble something. "I couldn't believe I'd said it. . . . Then I listened to myself say it again. And again and again. . . .'*Please, God, help me.*' I was praying. Asking. Begging. For help. . . . And I thought to myself: '*Me? Asking God? Begging God? Praying?*' I hadn't even thought about God since I was a boy. . . . And suddenly my heart was stilled. . . . I stopped trembling and twitching." As he rose to return home, he realized he was not alone, "I *thought I could do it now.* . . . It would be excruciatingly difficult, but with God's help, I thought I could do it." Eszterhas doesn't know whether to describe his experienced as God finding him, or him finding God. That day he accepted God's acceptance of himself. It was a day of grace.[5]

---

obstacles to God's grace are not all outside ourselves, and we are not merely passive victims of negative cultural influences. Our attitudes and choices separate us from God's love and keep God's grace from penetrating our lives.

All of the distractions, clutter, and willful complicities that keep us closed to grace contribute to a dis-ease of the spirit, the atrophy of the interior life, a distance from God and God's community. They cut us off from a good life and keep us from fruitful living. These elements of distance, both inherited and willful, are what Paul describes when he says, "sin increased" (Romans 5:20). Sin is brokenness and disconnectedness from God who created us.

Is there a way out, or a way through the obstacles, to the life God intends for us? How can we live fruitfully, happily, and meaningfully in the face of these recurring obstacles that separate us from God?

Opening to Grace

Beneath the daily surface life, there continually streams a spiritual dimension, an interior life, a richly sacred and eternal depth. In unexpected moments, events press us deeper than the superficial and invite us to search for answers to questions we haven't even thought to ask before. These moments mark the intersection of daily life and the life of the spirit, the interweaving of the mundane with the sacred, the intermingling of the immediate practical questions of getting along with the deeper questions of direction and purpose. In these moments of intrusion, events jar us into encounter with the deeper mysteries, and we may perceive God's grace reaching out to us.

Some of those moments include the birth of a child; when our children leave home for college, military service, or to work; a serious health threat or accident; the death of a family member or close friend; a national tragedy or natural disaster; a painful reversal at work or an unanticipated success; the start or end of a relationship. In all of these, we find ourselves exploring the question of what lasts.

Such events interrupt our surface existence with penetrating and life-changing impact. They cause us to face questions that the tangibles of a materialist culture or the certainties of reason do nothing to help us understand. We yearn for answers that cannot be provided by how much money we have, what kind of car we drive, or what newest celebrity gossip we know. Tangible, transient, and surface satisfactions cannot imbue our lives with the meaning we thirst for. These moments of reflection represent the intrusion into our lives of eternity and its questions, the gentle tapping on our shoulder of angels, the whispers of the Spirit. These moments create openings, make us aware of our yearning, and place us in a posture of curiosity and desire. They make us willing to open the door to God's love and ready to receive what God's grace may mean for our lives.

What's the purpose and end for which we were created? What is trustworthy and true? Who am I? How does God fit in to it all?

The answers do not come from outside of us. We never earn enough, do enough, or achieve enough to guarantee happiness. We do not become what God created us to be simply by more activity, faster motion, working harder, or having more stuff. More intensity on these external activities does not satisfy the soul.

And contrary to self-help books, the good life cannot come from inside us by our own efforts either. We do not achieve it by trying harder, pushing further, pulling ourselves up by our own bootstraps. Self-love, self-absorption, and self-focus do not take us there.

Happiness, meaning, and contribution come from connection to the source of life, from the grace we've become accustomed to closing out and denying by our distraction, clutter, and complicity. The door we've been closing on God's grace has been shutting us off from what we need the most.

The good life comes from the practice of hospitality toward God, opening ourselves to God, and making room in our hearts for the gift-like transformation God's love makes possible. Happiness results from patterns of living that draw us closer to God and one another, from practices that open and reopen the connections that bind us to God and to the community. We flourish as we learn to love and be loved, and to serve and be served. Flourishing comes from the sheer volume of human relationships that grace our lives; fruitful living results from an outward focus, from demonstrably loving others through the offering of ourselves to make a difference. Love changes everything.

Hospitality toward God opens us to new life. In the practice of making space for God in our hearts again and again, we accept God's gift of new life.

Mitch

Mitch grew up with no faith background. His alcoholic father was arrested for stealing money and was discovered having an extramarital affair, causing Mitch to have to change schools as a consequence of his parents' divorce. Mitch lost his friends, the job he loved, and his place on the baseball team. He developed a violent temperament, ran with rough characters, and made his own way in a tough world of sports, drinking, and hard living. During his early twenties, he lived with a seething anger toward his father that moved through his soul like a slow-moving river. His envy toward others ate at him, for the advantages they had received which he had been denied. He was angry about things that would never be resolved.

Mitch developed a tough veneer that hid any deeper sense of compassion. He had no faith, no church, no God, and no positive models for how to handle his life. He worked as a truck driver until he saved enough money to pay his way through college. He flirted with drug and alcohol abuse, but by sheer personal determination, he didn't get pulled irretrievably into these habits.

Mitch met a young woman who was committed to her faith. In preparation for their marriage, he had several conversations with her pastor. He came to respect the pastor, to learn from him, and to look forward to their times together. When Mitch married, he decided that he would "try church." "Is this for real?" was the inner question he wrestled with during his early hesitating steps toward faith. For months he attended with his wife, finding the worship service a confusing litany of language and images and prayers. He felt like an outsider, but he was determined to make it work. He and his wife connected with a Sunday school class for young couples. Mitch was invited to help at a community soup kitchen that serves the homeless, and he accepted. He was invited to help with the finance committee, and then with the trustees. He found these strangely satisfying, but he continued to feel turned off by small-minded attitudes and cliquishness. Mitch began to read the Bible, to experiment with praying, to volunteer a little more here and there. He helped with the youth ministry, especially the sports and outdoor activities. He particularly offered himself to work with the difficult kids.

Mitch experienced a deepening of his faith through the weekend adult retreat called *Walk to Emmaus*. He committed to the in-depth DISCIPLE Bible study, and eventually became a Bible study teacher himself, especially effective at gathering younger men who had never had any experience in studying Scripture. He offered himself as a team leader for hands-on service projects to build and repair homes for people in poverty. Through his nonjudgmental approach toward people, he became instrumental in helping many unchurched people get involved in various ministries.

Mitch's language is still rough, his manner brusque, and his approach to church and tolerance for protocol are, shall we say, less traditional. He relates well to professionals, feels like one of the boys among hardworking folk—oil riggers, ranch hands, and construction crews. When someone is going through a difficult time, he gives them his phone number and tells them to call him anytime, anywhere, and he'll come. Mitch believes the church really does change lives.

By the grace of God, Mitch has become someone different from the life that was scripted for him. Through faith in Christ, formed and cultivated through fifteen years of worship, learning, and service, Mitch has found the power to avoid the destructive impulses that undid his father and derailed his family of origin. By the practice of daily submitting himself to Christ, Mitch has come to a place he could never imagine—a sense of satisfaction and contribution, of making a difference and doing good in the lives of others.

The Apostle Paul writes, "So if anyone is in Christ, there is a new creation: everything old has passed away; see, everything has become new!" (2 Corinthians 5:17).

Mitch is a new creation. Over time, he has arrived at a place he never would have come to on his own. He is a radically different person from what he would have been had he never walked the path of faith in Christ.

Look back over Mitch's story and notice the many signs of receptivity, moments when he could have said *No*, but instead said *Yes* on the spiritual journey. Agreeing to meet with the pastor and to attend church with his wife, overcoming the awkwardness of worship, attending a young couples class, volunteering to help with the soup kitchen, initiating Bible study, experimenting with prayer—each of these became a steppingstone, a building block toward growth in Christ. Each was a sign of his hospitality toward God and of a willingness to allow God to enter in. At each key point, he received God, opened himself to the spiritual life, and welcomed God to play a larger role in his life. Following Christ has been a continuing lifelong process of opening his heart to God.

Practicing Radical Hospitality Toward God

The personal practice of Radical Hospitality begins with accepting God's love for us offered through Christ, and deciding to let that gracious love make a difference in our lives. It's an attitude; a mindset; an openness to spiritual things; a willingness to listen, perceive, and receive God's presence and initiative. The decision to receive God marks the start of our own journey and soul work, the first step toward a dynamic and vibrant life with God. It involves the critical decision, "Will I open the door to the spiritual life or leave it closed? Will I listen for God, invite God into my heart, and allow God's grace to shape my life, or not?" This receptivity expresses a willingness, a submission, a yearning. It involves a desire to put ourselves into God's hands, to be shaped into something new that we cannot now see. When we adopt this attitude of acceptance, and say *Yes* to God's initiating grace, we begin down a path that is presently unknown to us and that only becomes knowable as time unfolds. We say *Yes* to being a disciple, a learner and follower, trusting that as surely as others have been changed and shaped by this critical decision, so shall we.

Receptivity

Mary Ann describes spiritual receptivity this way: "You clear a space for the Spirit's voice, and close the door to as many other voices as possible—things to be done, people to meet, anxiety, guilt, duty. These are always pushing. You slide closed the door for a few moments. Listening for God takes persistence. The still, small voice is hard to recognize. But if you sit there long enough, something will happen. Peace, a letting go, a centering. An opening. If I practice it every day, I get better at it."

The personal practice of Radical Hospitality continues and is sustained with deliberate behaviors, the pursuing of a deepening relationship with God through practices that place us in the most advantageous position to continue to welcome Christ and make room for grace. Radical Hospitality toward God involves both the attitude of receptivity and intentional practice.

We intuitively know that connection, meaning, and contribution come from cultivating the interior life, the spiritual life, life with God. Something inside wants to be healed and to become whole. Something within knows that there is more than the surface existence. There is an inner wanting and waiting beyond conscious awareness, a curiosity, a ripeness and readiness to receive. God's grace (*prevenient* grace, as Wesley calls it, that makes ready our responses to God's offering of love before we even realize it), prepares us to accept that we are accepted, to say *Yes*, and to begin the journey.

Open the Door

"Listen! I am standing at the door, knocking; if you hear my voice and open the door, I will come in to you and eat with you, and you with me." (Revelation 3:20)

People who cultivate receptivity look for ways to invite God in rather than to close God out; they deliberately seek to say *Yes* to the promptings of the Spirit rather than to deny or avoid them.

They regularly ask for God's help, simply, humbly, and in no special language but their own. They desire God's presence.

They make space in their lives, room in their hearts, and time in their schedules to focus on interior work. Nurturing the spirit becomes as essential as feeding the body; soul work becomes as important as physical exercise. They open hearts and minds to God.

They invite interruptions by God into their lives, interventions of the Spirit, unexpected opportunities for doing what is life-giving. They look for sightings of the Spirit's work, evidence of God prompting love, service, generosity, sacrifice. They learn to perceive God.

People who demonstrate the quality of hospitality toward God are curious about God, spirituality, and the interior life. They desire to *know God* rather than merely to know *about God*.

Those who practice receptivity to God enjoy the exploration of the spiritual life, and embrace following Jesus as an adventure. They delight in new learning. They do not view religion as a burden, a mere duty, or as something that weighs heavy. Spirituality lifts them up.

The word *radical* intensifies the notion of receptivity. *Radical* means "outside the norm, drastically different from ordinary practice," and so it connotes giving priority and intentionality to receiving God into our lives. *Radical* derives from the word "root," and describes a profound, deep-rooted receptivity. Those who practice *Radical Hospitality* invite God into the core of their existence; seeking God becomes a fundamental and defining element of their existence.

Many of us approach the spiritual life the way we would an interesting hobby or constructive pastime, like fishing, gardening, golfing, or belonging to a book club. Being Christian comprises a small part of our identity. We attend church when it's convenient, we pick up some helpful insights and enjoy the people, and we serve on committees to help the organization run smoothly. Church, religion, and the spiritual life provide some benefit; but we remain puzzlingly remote from real interior work, mystery, or notions of grace. Practicing religion in this way *confirms* something about ourselves rather than *transforming* the nature of who we are. Religion is not really a power for living; it is an appendage to an otherwise harried and hectic schedule. Religion is more about attending church than following Christ. For many of us, personal prayer is incidental to the flow of life; serving others is something we do to be a faithful part of the team; contributing money involves doing our fair share. It's not that we close the door on God, we just haven't made much effort to seriously receive God fully into our lives.

Those people we admire because they display a depth, passion, integrity, and wisdom forged by a dynamic and vibrant faith have not taken the spiritual life so casually. At some fundamental point, they decided to receive God, to offer a hospitality that goes the second mile—an uncommon, *radical* hospitality toward God. Instead of going to visit God for an hour each week they bring God home with them, giving God place, priority, devotion. They explore the interior life. They reach for God and open themselves to God's reaching for them. They internalize faith for themselves, a faith that isn't perfunctory or empty, but which is a dynamic force in their lives. They open themselves to God in a radical way. They have said *Yes*, and *Yes* again, and they are immensely richer for doing so.

Even with many years of church experience, many of us may find ourselves still standing on the front porch of the life that is possible in Christ because we've never fully entered in. Or to change the metaphor, we may have left God standing on the front porch of our lives without fully receiving him. We've left undiscovered the "immeasurable riches of God's grace," "abundant life," and "a peace that surpasses all understanding."

People who practice Radical Hospitality toward God move beyond a tentative willingness to sample faith; they actively demonstrate an intentional receptivity to God. They make critical decisions because of their relationship with God. They allow God to become a principal part of their life and they become part of God's life. They lay open their hearts.

They *want* God to change them, to make them anew. A God-related life becomes an important stabilizing and orienting force. Growing in Christ becomes an objective.

People who practice receptivity realize that the spiritual journey requires deliberate, continuing cooperation with God. They practice, repeat, and deepen the core essentials that open themselves to God. The Christian life is more than knowledge about Jesus; it is a lifestyle to be mastered.

Receptivity means that the question, "Am I pleased with my life?" is matched and balanced with the question, "Is my life pleasing to God?" Rather than seeking something from God, they seek God.

They realize that deepening the spirit does not come quickly, that following Jesus can be inconvenient, and that gradually surrendering control to God is uncomfortable. They don't cling to the fantasy that spiritual maturity, satisfaction, and contribution fall into place easily. Saying *Yes* to grace empowers them and strengthens them to say *No* to many other things.

People who practice Radical Hospitality realize that opening themselves to God also involves opening themselves to the community of faith.

They are resilient and persistent, and they are not afraid to wrestle with God. Even when they are more keenly aware of God's absence than of God's presence, they persevere in the trust that in their searching, they are found.

They live with a less anxious attitude. In opening themselves to God's grace, they receive their validation. They are loved once, finally, and forever by God in Christ. By accepting God's love for them, nothing remains conditional, ambiguous, or incomplete about their ultimate worth. They build their house upon a rock.

They strive to love the things God loves, to want the things God wants, to find happiness in the things God gives, to find meaning in God's work. They seek first God's kingdom, and all else follows from that.

Accept that you are accepted. The first step toward fruitful living involves saying *Yes* to God's unconditional love toward us. God's love changes everything. The opening of ourselves to God's grace stimulates a passionate desire *to love God in return*, and this takes us to the second practice of fruitful living, Passionate Worship.

Questions for Reflection

• When have you experienced a time in your life when love changed you? Did this experience come to you suddenly and consciously or in more subtle ways? How did it change you?

• How have you felt God's unconditional love? Has it shaped your desire to do personal soul work? How do you understand the phrase "struck by grace"?

• Through what persons or events have you experienced the initiating quality of God's love? How did you allow God in? When have you said *Yes* to God's initiating grace rather than *No*, and what difference has this made for you?

- How do you compare the inner happiness that comes from God's Spirit with the happiness defined by the culture? What personal values or practices help you cultivate the good life?

- Where do you experience silence in your life? How do you feel about silence? What about it refreshes or reinvigorates you? What do you learn from it?

- What obstacles or distractions do you strive to overcome in order to fully receive God's love?

- How do your present patterns of living invite God in or cause you to avoid the spiritual life?

- When did you last evaluate your relationship with God? How are you closed to God's grace, and how are you open? What steps can you take to reshape your life toward greater receptivity?

CHAPTER TWO
Loving God in Return

The Practice of Passionate Worship

"You shall love the Lord your God with all your heart, and with all your soul, and with all your strength, and with all your mind; and your neighbor as yourself." —Luke 10:27

Linda was in her early forties when her husband died, leaving her the task of raising two young children by herself. Neither her own family nor her husband's were church people, and she regarded Christianity with skepticism and Christians with suspicion. A few years after her husband's death, her daughters began attending youth activities at a church with their friends. Today, they were singing in the youth choir at the Sunday service, and Linda wanted to be present to support them.

With no church background, attending worship was daunting to her. When she walked in the door, several people offered greetings, shook her hand, and gave her leaflets. She wasn't sure where she was supposed to go and so she stood awkwardly watching the flow of people. As she entered the sanctuary, almost every pew already had people sitting at the ends, and she wasn't sure if she was supposed to step over them or ask them to move down to make room for her. She felt utterly self-conscious about every step she took. But she persevered and found a place near the back.

As the time for the service approached, music began and people quieted down. She sorted through the announcements about upcoming events. Some piqued her curiosity—a recovery workshop, a financial management class, a Habitat for Humanity project—and others remained a mystery to her, their purpose hidden behind acronyms she didn't understand, such as the Acts 28 Team, the Keystone Class, and an Alpha-Omega Circle meeting. A pastor began to speak, and the people around her responded in unison; then everyone stood and began to sing. Neither the tune nor the words were familiar to her, and she felt awkward following the music. For several minutes everything seemed a confusing mix of announcements, greetings, quotes from Scripture, and moving around. During the prayers, someone mentioned a family by name that had lost a loved one and requested prayers for them. There was silence as people throughout the sanctuary focused on the grieving family. Linda remembered how alone she felt when her husband had died, and she wondered how it must feel to be surrounded by people who are praying for you. "What do the prayers do?" she wondered. She felt moved by the compassion of the gesture.

At last the youth choir moved forward, and she saw her daughters singing with their friends. A sense of parental satisfaction surged through her as she listened. The refrain was beautiful and catchy. She liked it. Later, the pastor told a story about a shepherd leaving the flock behind to search for the sheep that had gone astray. He said that the sheep had "nibbled its way lost," and Linda smiled at the line. That's how we get lost from God, the pastor said. We don't intend to, but we go from one tuft of grass to another until we end up somewhere we never imagined. And yet God loves us and searches for us and never gives up on any one of us. While Linda wasn't sure what she believed about God, the message made her think about her own life.

As the service ended, the mother of one of her daughters' friends came up to Linda and apologized for not noticing her sooner, gave her a gentle hug, and said how glad she was to see her. "Next time you're here, let's sit together," the woman said. Something washed over Linda in that moment that was sudden and profound. The words touched her. She had never imagined returning for worship before that moment. As if a thread of grace had been cast across a great chasm, she felt a connection ever so tenuous and yet full of promise. She returned to her car and sat there for several minutes. "What do I do with this?" she asked herself. "What just happened?" The refrains of her daughters' voices were running through her mind, she was actually praying for a grieving family she didn't even know, she was thinking about that sheep nibbling its way lost, and she was smiling about the invitation to return.

A Thread of Grace

"I always thought 'I'm praying for you' was a toss-away phrase, a polite way of expressing care when we don't know what else to say . . . then my father had a heart attack," Stephanie says. "A coworker said she would pray for me. She pulled out a notebook and wrote down my father's name. Later in the evening she called me to ask how I was doing. In the midst of the fear and uncertainty, I didn't feel alone anymore. Someone genuinely cared."

Prayer casts threads of grace across chasms of disconnection, loneliness, fear, and pain. Prayer weaves people back into community and rebinds them to the source of life.

Worship

Worship expresses our love for God, our devotion to the creator, redeemer, and sustainer of life. Our response to God's great love for us is to love others and to serve them, and also to express our adoration to God. We love God in return. We open ourselves to God's Spirit so we can see the world through God's eyes. Worship involves voluntarily setting time aside to focus on God's will rather than our own agenda, to receive God's word rather than merely giving our point of view. We offer ourselves anew to God's purposes rather than trying to fit God neatly into our own goals. A sustained pattern and practice of worship lends coherence, meaning, depth, and connection to our lives. Worship reconfigures our interior lives and aligns us with the life of Christ. Worship connects us to God.

Worship changes us. Understanding the meaning of worship requires looking beyond *what people do* to see with the eyes of faith *what God does*. God uses worship to crack open closed hearts, reconcile broken relationships, renew hope, restrain harmful arrogance, heal wounded souls, shape personal decisions, interrupt destructive habits, stimulate spiritual growth, and transform lives. God reshapes the human soul through worship.

Since ancient times, people have gathered to seek God through prayer, story, music, song, fellowship, and mutual compassion. *Synagogue* means "to bring together." God lives in the people gathered in devotion and covenant. And the Latin word *ecclesia*, the root of our word for church, means "called out of the world." God calls us out of the ordinary life of work, family, and leisure into the presence of the sacred so that we can develop the spiritual resources that guide and sustain fruitful living.

Worship is the reason God liberated the Hebrew people from the oppressions of slavery. God spoke to Moses, saying, "Release my people so they can worship me" (Exodus 8:1, *The Message*). God desires our devotion.

Jesus presents the highest of God's desires this way, "That you love the Lord your God with all your passion and prayer and muscle and intelligence—and that you love your neighbor as well as you do yourself" (Luke 10:27, *The Message*). Heart, mind, soul, and strength—in worship we offer all to God in love.

Worship provides the most likely setting for the change of heart and mind we describe as *justification*, the moment of conscious awareness and decision that involves our receiving God's grace through Christ, confessing our need for God, accepting God's pardon, and turning our lives toward God and away from former ways. Jesus tells the story of the Pharisee and the tax collector entering the Temple (Luke 18:9-14). The Pharisee is so full of himself that he is unable to open himself to God. The tax collector, consciously aware of his brokenness and spiritual emptiness, genuinely offers his heart to God. Jesus says the tax collector leaves a different person than when he came in. He is *justified*—by grace his life freshly aligns with God. He discovers a new relationship with God through open-hearted worship and devotion to God.

In the Gospels, Jesus and his followers regularly attend temple, read from Scripture, speak of giving, practice prayer, retreat to God, give thanks, and observe the sabbath. Worship becomes their natural breath. Worship strengthens them for ministry. Living in God involves returning God's love.

Why Does Worship Matter?

Orienting Ourselves Toward God

What happens in worship, and why is it important? First, worship is the way we orient ourselves toward God. If God's unconditional love is the pivotal truth of life, how do we set aside time to focus on God, to receive God's love, and to love God in return? Worship connects us to God and to other people who also self-consciously choose to orient themselves toward God. God desires a relationship with us, and in response to God's seeking us, worship is our way of seeking God, our reaching upward to God's reaching downward.

Discovering the Transcendent

Second, worship fosters our relationship to the transcendent, spiritual aspects of life. We temporarily push other more tangible and mundane things aside to discover more mysterious and sacred elements and to approach them with awe and openness. We put spiritual and relational things first.

Many of life's most critical questions cannot be answered through more information, with better science, or by linear modes of intellectual exploration. Questions of meaning, purpose, love, suffering, connection, life, death, and hope require a more elastic and searching form of knowledge. Spiritual insight, while as true and eternal as the laws of gravity, requires grasping certainties that are not describable principally by fact or science, but by experience, trust, and grace. When we gather to deal with facets of life for which there are no easy or explicit answers, we find ourselves exploring the wonderfully transcendent parts of our existence. In the *beyondness* of silence, prayer, reflection, music, embrace, ritual, and community, we discover insight, sustenance, beauty, and awe. Like a breeze—felt but never seen—the Spirit feeds our wild need for wonder, our essential search for meaning.

Human beings are not oriented merely by one sense or two, but by many. Imagine a room full of people; one third understand and speak only German, another third only Spanish, and another third only English. If we speak only one language, we leave two-thirds of the people unaddressed, and we cannot receive the gift of their insight and knowledge. If we want to communicate with all of them and receive the resources they offer us, we will have to learn to communicate in other languages.

Likewise with the interior life: perhaps only one third of the knowledge and wisdom to live meaningfully is reducible to and reachable by conscious, linear, rational thought. This we learn through words, sermons, and the sharing of ideas. But another third of insight and experience that expands our sense of meaning, motivation, and connection comes to us through music, silence, movement, liturgy, and a host of other means. These are truths we absorb in ways beyond our conscious awareness. Nevertheless, they form us, strengthen us, and connect us to God and one another. For instance, it is a mystery that breaking bread and sharing wine makes us one and forms us into the body of Christ, but it does. Communion is an outward sign of an inward grace, a visible reminder of a mysteriously spiritual truth. Receiving bread and wine, viewing artistry in stained glass, kneeling alongside others, bowing our heads, singing songs that lift the soul, meditating upon the cross, offering our gifts—these feed us and form us with truths beyond verbal articulation. And another third of insight and truth comes through the experience of being together with others, our sense of belonging. By praying for one another, serving and receiving Communion, and harmonizing our voices in song, we discover the grace of community. Navigating the unknown and uncertain seas of life—of suffering and healing, of disconnection and reconciliation, of life and death—we realize through worship that we are all on the same ship sailing toward the same port. Worship grants us a coherent sense of belonging, of purpose, and of future.

Practicing worship is like learning other languages that open us to the full resources of the spiritual life. God's transcendent love pulls us out of ourselves, stretches us, and takes us beyond where we could possibly arrive on our own. Realities beyond conscious reach become accessible to us. God is present in silence, ritual, music, and movement as we grasp the powerlessness of our words to describe the meaning and grace of community.

God's presence fills the room, embracing us, creating a sense of belonging discernable to those who receive it, known to us without our seeing it, present before we consciously ask for it or realize it. Through worship we rise up and soar.

Engaging the Spirit

Third, worship is our way of putting ourselves in the most advantageous place for engaging the Spirit. While God is present in all of life, it is through worship that we purposefully search for God and become acutely aware of God's presence. We give our attention to God, and focus on God's revelation rather than merely our own. We listen for God with greater intentionality. God may be present anywhere—including at the golf course or on our back patio or in the great outdoors. However, our reason for being in those other places is not explicitly to search for God, to notice God, listen for God, or open our souls to God's heart and God's people.

Worship represents a regular appointment with the sacred, a planned encounter, a scheduled time and place to connect. We arrive with souls prepared, minds ready, and hearts open, and our anticipation makes worship different from other times. Our singing and praying together represent a conscious choice to form a rhythm of engagement with the spiritual elements of life that balances our engagement with the world. We could spend our Sundays in a thousand different ways, many of them positive and helpful. We could choose to work, but instead of being materially productive today we choose to focus on God. We could choose to play, sleep, or exercise; but instead we've decided that our relationship with God is of such importance that we've set those things aside to attend to this pivotal relationship.

Bringing Us Back to Ourselves

Fourth, worship brings us back to ourselves. People frequently describe worship as the activity during their week that centers them, grounds them, connects them, or anchors them. All these words reveal the risk we feel of losing touch, becoming distracted, unfocused, and disconnected, or living haphazard and harried lives rather than feeling rooted and grounded in what really matters. In worship we "sing our shadows home," as an ancient Native American story tells. We come back to ourselves.

Impressions of Grace

"When I visited her at her nursing home, she no longer recognized me. She did not even know where she lived, and she seemed quite agitated. It was disheartening," Ann says of her grandmother with Alzheimer's. "But when someone began to play 'Amazing Grace' on the piano, my grandmother's face glowed, she sang the words from memory, tears fell from her eyes, and she settled into her seat with a sense of calm. I was astonished, and grateful."

Worship runs deep. Music, prayers, and liturgy leave lifelong impressions that lend coherence, support, and connection beyond what we can comprehend.

Worship carves out a time to focus on the larger questions of life, of end and purpose. It lifts our eyes beyond the immediate and tangible to look at life from a wider perspective. We have time to reflect, anticipate, reprioritize, and to push the reset button in our spiritual lives when we might otherwise veer off course from our most vital relationships. A tragic undercurrent of our culture is how many people feel lost within their families, within their communities, within their world. Worship provides purpose, correction, and a sense of community. Worship helps us catch our breath, prepare, reunite, and renew. Worship provides a way by which we let ourselves be found, a way to find God, and to find ourselves.

Through prayers, music, sermon, and sacrament, we remember (literally, *re-member*), enfolding ourselves once more into the body of people who follow Jesus. Worship reminds us that we belong to God and to one another, and this sense of belonging is essential for our spiritual well-being. The repeated metaphors of unity—one body, one bread, one baptism, one God, one family in which we all are sisters and brothers in Christ—weave us into a community of mutual care and compassion that sustains us. We bind ourselves to one another and to God during worship so that during the challenging times throughout the week, we do not become unbound. In worship, we love because we are loved.

The purpose of worship does not begin and end with what human beings do; worship is the means God uses to accomplish God's purposes in the human heart and in the community of Christ. God is active in worship even when we are not. God speaks to us. God accomplishes the continuing reconciliation of the world through worship.

Imagine worship from God's point of view. What does God seek through our gathering to love and serve God? Does God need our praise? God desires our praise because by praising God we open our hearts to God's love and direct our hearts toward the following of God's ways. God's desire for our praise reveals God's desire for what is best for us. In worship, God offers a setting for us to confess our brokenness, receive pardon, and relieve our guilt. God works with us to reconstruct a pathway that leads to greater fullness. God plants seeds in our heart and soul with the anticipation that some of these will take root and grow within us. In worship, God, the gardener of the soul, clears the weeds, waters the seeds of hope and courage, helps us blossom in love, and flourish into wonderfully fruitful lives. Worship itself, and every element of it, is a means of grace, a way for God to accomplish our re-creation.

Passionate Worship

People enter worship with eagerness, yearning, and devotion. They offer themselves passionately, and they anticipate God's presence. "My soul longs, indeed it faints, for the courts of the LORD" (Psalm 84:2). They seek God. Passionate Worship describes the practice of those for whom worship is not merely routine or performance, but a means of connecting to God. Passionate Worship feeds a dynamic, vibrant, fruitful relationship with God.

Passion means full of life, involving our whole selves—mind, body, and spirit. People who love God passionately enter worship with eagerness, anticipation, expectation, a yearning for God. They are drawn by their love for God rather than by feeling expected to attend a social function. Passionate Worship has as its source and purpose the desire to connect ourselves to God and to God's people. Passionate Worship is authentic rather than contrived, from the heart rather than merely going through motions. *Passion* means inflamed with love, and refers to our desire to open ourselves entirely to God, inviting God's Spirit to permeate us completely. Through Passionate Worship, we love God in return, and through our continuing practice we stay in love with God.

Worship settles us in God, and anchors us in Christ. *Passion* connotes doing something with such fullness of feeling that our love pushes us through all the hesitations and doubts and setbacks that might otherwise give us pause. Passionate Worship expresses our desire to put God at the center of our lives.

Without a Sound

Imagine that you were unable to hear the sounds of worship in your congregation and you could only observe with your eyes. What would you see in the faces of people as they arrived? Would you see warmth, receptivity, eagerness? Boredom, anxiety, impatience? Would people appear self-absorbed or focused on others? Would they appear happy to be present or anxious to leave? What would their body language and posture and responses to others reveal? What would people see in your eyes and by your behavior? Would they see grace?

In theology, *the Passion* refers to the complete outpouring of Jesus Christ, the offering of himself, even to death on a cross, in order to complete our relationship with God through Christ. In the Passion of Christ, we receive grace upon grace. The sacrifice of Christ—Jesus' life, death, and resurrection—is the turning point of our relationship with God and the center-point of our worship. In the Passion of Christ, God reaches for us. In our passionate response, we reach for God.

The path to fruitful living, to discovering the riches of the spiritual life, involves practicing worship seriously and with committed consistency, rather than attending worship haphazardly, infrequently, and without enough consistency to feel at home and confident about worshipping God. Truly cultivating a relationship with God requires a conscious effort to make the practice of worship a lifelong priority.

The Mystery of Worship

Any attempt to completely describe worship falls short. In ways we cannot fully comprehend, we practice visible and tangible behaviors which result in our feeling sustained, grounded, forgiven, connected, motivated to make better choices, and called to serve others. How that happens often remains beyond conscious awareness or description. Worship is mystery.

Why does repeating the history of God's grace, praying, giving God thanks, kneeling with others, and receiving a piece of bread and a taste of grape juice affect us? I have received the sacrament of Holy Communion and presided over its liturgy thousands of times, and yet I feel utterly inadequate explaining why and how participating in this simple ritual affects the human spirit. That the breaking of bread makes us one and that the receiving of it makes us whole are true, but how this works is beyond my capacity to comprehend or explain. It is mystery.

At times I'm overwhelmed by the immediate sense of the sacrament's power; it consciously and presently affects me. As I'm repeating the words, receiving bread, or watching other people do so, I discern a palpable sense of being deeply affected. An elderly couple support each other in their kneeling and rising; a family with young children huddle together to take the bread; varied languages and accents carry the whispered responses; people step forward carrying unbearable grief, secret joy, unspoken remorse, and newfound resolve. Watch those who step forward one after another, and meditate on all that their lives represent. What do all these people have in common? All of them remember God's love in Christ, taking Christ's broken body into themselves, and temporarily orient themselves once more toward the ultimate revelation of God's love for each of us. They take Christ's life as their own. Worship blesses us.

People stepping forward to receive the sacrament become a fine tapestry interwoven by the Holy Spirit into one people. They are one with each other, one with Christ, and one in ministry to the world. In this simple act, they become community; communion with Christ becomes real, and they experience a sense of belonging not merely to the people present in the room but to all those who have gone before and who will follow. They form and reinforce an identity and spiritual bond with all who voluntarily receive into themselves the sacrificial love of God in Christ. Once more they become new persons in Christ.

Every single hour since the middle of the first century, somewhere in our world people have taken bread and broken it, calling it the body of Christ, and have given it to one another to remember Christ. They have used roughly the same words and told the same story in hundreds of languages. When we break the bread, we join a company of people that extends around the entire world as well as back in history, forward into the future, and upward to eternity. Even if we repeat it a million times, we never fully comprehend its meaning and impact. It is mystery.

There are times I can sense the unifying presence of the Holy Spirit in the sacrament as surely as I feel the bread in my fingers. Other times I feel like I'm repeating a perfunctory ritual and reading words by rote. People with tears streaming down their faces at the spiritual power of the moment kneel alongside others who roll their eyes at the seeming nonsense of it all. How can this be? The bread itself does not change its substance, and afterward remains merely bread as beforehand. But through our remembering Christ and his conscious commitment to the salvation of the world and by inviting the Spirit's presence, we change the use of these ordinary elements. As their purpose changes, we are changed. Through the eyes of faith, these are no longer merely ordinary bread and wine but the body and blood of Christ. We're taking Christ into us as God is taking us into the body of Christ. Is the change in our lives perceptible? Sometimes yes. Sometimes no. Yet, by repeating the sacrament, the practice has a mysteriously formative impact on our lives. The ritual becomes a means of grace, a revealing in tangible form of an intangible and invisible truth.

Truth, love, and creativity always come from places we never fully comprehend. By feeding the mind, heart, and soul by these motions and words, we give the Spirit space to play, to move around the deep places inside us and shake us up, to take root and to expand within us. Thoughts that weren't there in us before are now there. Beyond conscious awareness, something below the surface goes on, something real and life-changing. The regular repeating of the sacrament creates us anew.

A Converting Sacrament

While receiving the broken bread in his hands, Carl felt struck by the reconciling sacrifice of Christ. He thought about his brother with whom he had not spoken for more than five years, and the brokenness he sensed. In an unexpected moment of clarity, he realized how much responsibility he himself carried for the disconnection. "Life is too short, and someone has to take the first step," he thought. That afternoon, he phoned his brother and began a conversation. An uneasy and awkward beginning blossomed into a more comfortable pattern of phone calls over the months that followed. By reconnecting to his brother, Carl filled a part of himself that was empty.

Communion is not merely a *confirming* sacrament that reassures us of our belonging to the community of Christ; it is a *converting* sacrament God uses to reframe our hearts and redirect our behaviors.

Likewise with other sacraments and services, their effect and meaning are both mysterious and real. God loves us even before we represent God's grace with the sacrament of baptism; we give our hearts to Christ even before the confirming words we speak aloud; we belong to the body of Christ even without the membership pledge that makes our intentions known; a couple's love for each other is real prior to the wedding vows that make their covenant public; God receives our spirits whether we utter words of faith at the funeral or not. But in our saying and doing these things, deep invisible hopes and graces become tangible, visible, and public. Our highest yearnings and God's deepest desires rise up to expressible and accessible levels. Mysteriously, our rituals make all the more true what is already the case! They connect us to God.

Music is another aspect of worship that connects us with God. It is a mystery how music shapes the human spirit, but it does. Music makes us happy—to sing it, hear it, and share it. And music moves us to profound contemplation, reaching depths that are otherwise inaccessible by mere words or intentional reflection. Music helps

us say things we have trouble speaking in words. It offers a means
to proclaim our love for God that comes not only from the conven-
tional thoughts of our minds, but from the more emotive, heartfelt,
spontaneous parts in our souls. With music, we discover accents of
wonder and dimensions of awe that are otherwise inexpressible.
Music lifts us to God.

Music remains with us, embedding rhythms, tunes, and words
within us without our even knowing it. Music is a principal means
by which we explore, discover, and receive spirituality. Music opens
the door to the interior life and helps us bring God into daily life.

The melodies of European hymn writers, the rhythms of the people of Africa, the cadence of Native American influences, the
acoustic American folk sounds—all branches of the Christian family have used music to reach for God, to listen to God, and to praise
God. Slaves in America used music to bind their hearts to God and
one another, to inspire courage, to relieve suffering, and to express
their aspirations for freedom. Slaves found the passageway to
another reality through music, preaching, and worship. Music provided not an escape from but an embracing of reality that granted
a measure of spiritual freedom that paved the way to political freedom. Christians sing their way to new life.

Music, in its practical aspects, affects us by writing truths upon
our hearts in a manner that we carry with us wherever we go. We
learn the content of the faith more easily with the rhyme and
rhythm of lyrics and music. How many times we find the refrains
from recent worship replaying through our minds—*Amazing grace
how sweet the sound . . . Our God is an awesome God . . . Because he
lives I can face tomorrow . . .* Music makes spiritual truths poetic and
memorable. Music grants the pleasure and leisure to ruminate
unconsciously upon meanings long after we consciously repeat
them. When we leave worship, music goes with us and carries us
forward into the week.

Music has an undeniable unifying effect. Where else do non-
musicians join their voices with others to sing? Rarely outside of
national anthems and carols at Christmas parties do people experience singing together with others. We are unpracticed in the power
of singing together and what that means.

Singing together rehearses community. Sharing our individual
gifts leads to community outcomes that far exceed the sum of the

individual parts. Harmonizing voices reflects the harmony with others we seek in the world. Singing lifts us out of ourselves and binds us together.

Music touches places in our soul where no sermon could ever reach, penetrating where no words could ever go. Music puts spirit into us, raises us up, and brings us soberly to face our own mortality. Sermons inform us in important ways, but music takes us on a trip to the other side of our brains where fact, data, rationality, and objectivity end like a pier extending over a sea with unfathomable depths. Music allows us to jump into the deeper waters of the soul and into aspects of community and grace that we cannot begin to consciously understand. Music caresses the unconscious and subconscious and preconscious parts of the human psyche. Why would we not be curious to discover and recover its power? Music helps us attend to something both primitive and present, both elemental and sophisticated. It's hard to imagine the spiritual life without music and the world it opens to us. And yet how it affects us remains a mystery. Music is a means of grace.

Perhaps the greatest mystery involves how the affectionate attention to ordinary things in worship—prayer, music, liturgy, Scripture, sacrament, word, offering, fellowship—reveals a beauty, depth, meaning, and coherence that opens us to the discovery and rediscovery of grace in everyday situations throughout the week. Worship trains our attentiveness to God, attunes us to noticing the Spirit. Not only does it help us perceive things anew during the worship service itself, it helps us see things in everyday life we never saw before. Our quality of attention to God improves; and we begin to see God's work, sense God's presence, and discern God's call more naturally. In worship, we give our hearts to God. One hour each week changes all the other hours of our week.

Worship is mystery, and part of our task is not merely to wrestle with the mystery or seek to avoid it, but to embrace it and receive it.

Personal Worship and Devotion

Another way we express our love to God through worship is in our daily prayers and devotions. People who practice loving God in return carve out time in each day to intentionally focus on God, to express gratitude, offer private confession, and lift petitions and intercessions. Prayer at fixed times, such as morning prayers when rising, grace before meals, or evening prayers at the close of the day help us create a space in our lives for God. Daily habit provides the same restorative, centering, and encouraging quality to daily life that community worship adds to weekly life. Short devotional reading, reciting a prayer, or the simple observance of silence settles us in God. We orient ourselves a little each day toward God. Daily prayer blesses us.

We can't develop a meaningful relationship with someone if we don't spend time with them. The same is true with our relationship with God. Daily prayer and private worship is time with God.

Frequently, we cling too tightly to anger, blame, hate, hurt, grief, guilt, and sadness. How can we restore our souls, heal our brokenness, and relieve our fear? Daily prayer filters our experiences through our relationship with God. Through patterns of personal devotion, we perceive life differently, regulate negative emotions, and lift them up to God. Through prayer, we see even the most intransigent and painful experiences as pathways to new life. Prayer helps us face the darkness inside while reaching for the light. One kind of experience becomes something else entirely through prayer as we move toward transformation, resurrection, and a continuing rebirth. Prayer gives us courage to choose paths that lead to life.

Personal prayer changes our relationships with friends, coworkers, strangers, and even those toward whom we feel animosity. The places in ourselves that are most disconnected from God, when explored persistently and honestly in prayer, lead us also to reconciliation with others. We repair disconnection with others through soul work; inner peace reaps an outward harvest.

Daily personal devotion prepares us for community worship. God's ability to reach us increases as we cooperate with the Holy Spirit in making ready our souls to receive God's word. Personal prayer fosters eagerness for community worship.

Resistances to Worship

Someone new to following Jesus or with little experience may find starting or returning to a regular pattern of worship a daunting task. Stepping into a gathering of people who sing, pray, stand, sit, or kneel for reasons we don't understand makes us feel awkward. And yet this is true for any new experience—learning tennis, joining a fitness club, beginning a new friendship. We feel a little foolish, clumsy, and self-conscious before we develop a comfortable confidence that makes continuing on feel worthwhile. A nourishing pattern of worship takes time and commitment.

Any commitment exists in a context of competing obligations, habits, and interests. To move in one direction means forgoing other directions. To attend worship with frequency and consistency means reprioritizing time and making the effort. Worship results from intentionality.

Sometimes attending worship requires acting against the resistance, criticism, or ridicule of a spouse or friend. Seeking God is overtly countercultural in many contexts. Following Christ requires the capacity to handle the stress of going our own way and making our own decisions without the support of others we love. If you feel called to return to worship, do so. Do not wait for the day when everyone agrees to come with you. Your friends love the *old* you; they will love the *new* you as well, but it takes time for that to emerge, and we cannot let friends undermine our efforts to explore the spiritual life. Worship requires resolve.

Sometimes attending worship feels difficult because we are not sure we really believe all that following Jesus seems to involve. And yet beliefs emerge and rise to greater clarity through the practice of worship and by belonging to a community of faith. No one takes the first steps toward Christ by comprehending all the nuances of faith at once. At times, people worship, not to express something with absolute certainty, but in order not to remain altogether silent about what they intuitively feel: that they yearn for peace; that they desire to align themselves with what is good and just; and that they desire to serve others, explore spirituality, and learn to love. These motivate us even when we cannot express our underlying beliefs with clarity or in theological terms. Worship suggests trust.

Everyone also faces internal resistances, and most people backslide occasionally in their personal or public commitments to worship. Our faith life fluctuates between times of curiosity and tedium, exhilaration and ordinariness, doubt and rediscovery. By stepping back in and repeating familiar prayers both when they make perfect sense and when they puzzle us completely, worship anchors us. Making the effort to stay connected is difficult but important. When we start a fresh pattern of worship, everything in our life pulls against the new practice to restore the old habits that existed previously. The courage to start leads to the strength to continue. Worship takes persistence.

We worship because we love God. We do it to connect to other people. We do it to find ourselves. We discover a whole new world. Worship fosters joy, connection, self-understanding, and meaning. God desires to connect with us and to connect us to others. Worship lifts us, humbles us, motivates us, and pulls us out of ourselves. Worship fundamentally changes us.

As for all the practices, a pattern of passionate worship requires a surrendering, a yielding of ourselves and of our will, a giving up of some good things in order to attend to greater things. Surrender involves trust, openness, and vulnerability. Following Christ involves an incremental relinquishing of our control in order to allow God's Spirit to form us anew. To "have in us the mind that is in Christ" is a gradual process, a maturing, a becoming. There are no experts, only learners, and those who have stepped down the path a little farther than we have. We gradually feel less awkward, more connected, more confident in the face of the resistances, and immeasurably more aware of the blessings that accrue with falling in love with God. Worship God.

The Practice of Passionate Worship

People who practice Passionate Worship attend worship frequently and consistently until it becomes a valued and sustaining pattern for them. Worship becomes a priority and they shift schedules to attend when conflicts arise. They love worship because they love God.

They honor God by availing themselves of the sacraments, becoming familiar with the constituent parts of the worship service, receiving the musical offerings of the choir or band, and opening their minds to the Scriptures and sermon. They open themselves to God's Word as a means of loving.

They enter worship with hearts and minds prepared. They eagerly anticipate how God may connect to them. They read the Scriptures in advance. They pray for the pastor, the church staff, the musicians, and all who lead worship. They take notes when something strikes them so they can mull it over in private. They ask themselves, "What is God saying to me today through the songs, the Scripture and sermon, the sacrament, or the fellowship of others?" Loving God means listening for God.

People who practice Passionate Worship let music into their souls. They lift their voices in praise to God. They let themselves sing.

People who love worship offer their services to enhance the experience for others. If they are able, they sing in the choir or praise band, serve as ushers, greeters, lay readers, or Communion servers, or they help prepare the worship space. They create a sense of warmth and welcome for others. They influence an atmosphere of expectation. Worship is the most important hour of the week.

They carry their daily lives with them into prayer and worship, and carry worship and prayer with them into their daily lives. They live so that their whole life glorifies and praises God.

They are people of prayer. They pray in a style that sustains them. Some find a quiet time each morning and others do so at night; some take walks to orient themselves toward God and others meet with friends; some use printed prayers and devotions and others open themselves spontaneously; some kneel, others sit, and still others pray during exercise; some pray at home and others at the office. They make time to pray.

They read about prayer, learn about prayer, pray with others, and develop the habit of prayer. They practice prayer until it feels as natural as breathing. They teach their children to pray. They may keep a prayer list of people and concerns. Prayer for them becomes more than asking things of God. They listen for God and discern what God asks of them. They cultivate the gifts of silence and waiting. Clarity is born in spiritual stillness. They create times to pause, rest, listen, and prepare themselves for God. They pray without ceasing.

They love God, and they invest themselves wholeheartedly in cultivating their relationship with God. They let God reach them and change them through worship. They foster the spiritual life.

Helen

Helen grew up active in the Christian faith. At her baptism as an infant, her parents vowed to support her growth in grace. As a young girl, Helen loved worship. She learned songs in vacation Bible school, led youth services, and worshipped outdoors at summer camp. At confirmation, she committed herself to follow Christ. At her wedding, she and her husband made public their covenant before God. Helen adapted patterns of worship with each phase of her life, shaped by the activities of her children and her own changing needs. Frequently, Helen assisted with Communion, served as a lay reader of Scripture, worked as an usher, or volunteered for the worship committee.

She became one of those people to whom others instinctively turn for insight and counsel. She wore the mantel of spiritual encourager with great humility. She was even-tempered, warm, open, and gracious.

Helen loved Scripture, and each year would sign up to participate in Bible study. Helen's comments had a different quality to them, profoundly personal, reflective, and engaging. Scripture was not merely about people "over there, back then," but about our own lives. She'd quietly say, "I feel that God may be telling me something through this story . . ." She allowed herself to be shaped by God's Spirit.

For instance, a single sermon stimulated her to organize a prayer group. She and five of her friends met weekly for years to encourage one another's growth in Christ. In another sermon, she sensed God's call to initiate a literacy tutoring ministry among immigrant families. A service about tithing set her on the path of increased giving, and this inspired her to teach others the spiritual significance of generosity. Through a *Walk to Emmaus* retreat, she felt the Spirit prompt her to a deeper life of prayer and of teaching prayer. The retreat invigorated her love for Holy Communion, and she came to regard the sacrament as one of the most important practices of her spiritual life.

Helen's rich interior life overflowed into the lives of other people. At times she'd step into the church office and ask if she could pray with me. In stressful situations, she'd remind me, "Perhaps there's something God thinks you need to learn from this." Prayer, she'd remind me, was about desiring God, not just desiring something from God. Her soul work helped others with theirs.

She invited people into the life of the church, intuitively knowing the right things to say and do to make guests feel at home in worship. She made room in the church for strangers, becoming a friend and encourager.

Helen was diagnosed with cancer when she was in her mid-fifties. For two years she faced the uncertain and anguishing rhythm of progress and setback. All those people she had loved came back into her own life as caregivers and prayer partners. She grew weaker physically, but continued to strengthen everyone around. Friends and family gathered with her for a service of healing. They shared Communion and surrounded her with prayer. People found themselves overwhelmed by her graciousness, her sense of peace, and the ease by which she accepted death itself as a kind of grace. Her funeral was a celebration of life, an expression of gratitude to God for a life well-lived. Helen taught us how to live, and how to die.

Helen was deep-hearted, generous, grounded, and wise. She became that kind of person through a lifetime of worship.

Imagine if we could extract from Helen's life all the formative worship experiences that impacted her. Imagine if we could remove from her heart, mind, and soul all the thousands of worship services; tens of thousands of hymns, sermons, and prayers; the children's songs and campfire devotions. Imagine if we could take away the baptismal vows taken by her parents, the commitment she made at her confirmation, the covenant she embraced at her wedding, the renewal she experienced with the sacrament. Imagine if we could take away all the daily morning prayers she offered, the blessings before meals, the prayers she taught at the bedside of her children, the intercessions others offered for her. After extracting all these experiences from her life, who would she be?

We would not recognize her as the same person. The lifelong practice of loving God fundamentally changed her. Worship changed how she viewed herself and her relationship with God; it formed her sense of purpose and drew her toward others; through worship, God called her to make a difference in the world and she responded. In worship, she made the most critical decisions and commitments of her life. Worship gave her depth and coherence, a purpose that was irreplaceable, and that was only achievable by the path she took in following Christ. Her life was saturated with grace. Through worship, she became someone she otherwise never would have become.

The chapter began with Linda feeling awkward, and yet curious about worship. New to worship, she has yet to discover the rhythm, strength, and belonging that comes with the practice of loving God. We end with Helen, for whom worship was life. At whatever stage of faith we find ourselves, God uses worship to reach us, to change our hearts, and to make us God's own. Through worship, we reach for God in return, devoting ourselves with passion so that we begin to see the world through God's eyes. God loves us, and God uses our practice of loving God in return to form us into followers of Jesus Christ.

"I am the vine," Jesus said, "you are the branches" (John 15:5). Worship connects the branches to the vine, keeps us connected to the source of life, and helps us grow in Christ.

Through Radical Hospitality, we invite God into our lives and receive God's gracious love for us. Through Passionate Worship, we love God in return. God uses worship to change our hearts and minds. This creates in us a desire to grow in grace all the more, and this leads us to the next practice of fruitful living, Intentional Faith Development.

Questions for Reflection

- What are your earliest memories of worship? What made the greatest impression on you?

- Do you enjoy worship? What causes you delight? What sustains you in worship? What impacts you the most and what influences you the least?

- When was a time you felt connected to God in worship? When has a worship experience changed your heart and mind and provided you with fresh spiritual insights? What about worship refreshes and replenishes you?

- Think of an experience of Holy Communion that particularly moved you. What made it especially meaningful? How does Holy Communion shape your connection to God and God's people?

- Have you felt your spirit moved or lifted up to God by music in worship? How does singing make a difference in your spiritual life?

- What aspect of worship creates for you the greatest sense of cohesion and connection to others? What aspect expresses mystery?

- How do your daily prayers help you connect to God? How has praying with others helped you feel God's Spirit at work?

- When was a time you felt discomfort or resistance to the experience of worship? How do you work through this?

- How have you made worship a priority in your life? What changes would it take to make worship a higher priority?

CHAPTER THREE

Growing in Grace

The Practice of Intentional
Faith Development

*"Let us consider how to provoke one another to love and good
deeds, not neglecting to meet together, as is the habit of some,
but encouraging one another . . ." —Hebrews 10:24-25*

Rita attends to the last-minute details before people arrive. She
sets up the DVD and places her Bible, workbook, and notepad on the
recliner in her living room where she will lead tonight's session. As
she reviews her notes, Joel starts the coffee maker, mixes lemonade,
and sets out cookies he purchased at the bakery on the way home
from work. He carries chairs from the dinner table into their living
room. With the couch and the other furniture, everyone will have a
place, although a few people inevitably prefer to sit on the floor.

Rita and Joel teach an eight-week Bible study focused on the
parables of Jesus. Six years earlier, they began their own journey
into the exploration of Scripture. They'd been active in the congregation for several months when they responded to an invitation to
a series on Philippians. The study stoked their curiosity. Later they
belonged to the pastor's Bible study, a weekly series that focused
on the Scriptures the pastor used during worship. They enjoyed
the refreshing sense of friendship, but wanted something that
delved more deeply. The next year, they joined a DISCIPLE Bible
study, an in-depth, long-term study. They weren't sure how the
daily readings and the weekly meetings would work, especially
with teenagers at home, Rita's career, and Joel's travel; but they
tried it anyway. They loved it, and between classes, they found
themselves talking about the topics that came up in their readings.
They appreciated how closely they were growing to the others in
the group. "Belonging to that Bible study was one of the best things

we ever did. We began to feel comfortable with the Bible and to feel at home with other people in the congregation."

They continued to participate in Bible studies, usually together as a couple, but sometimes apart. They were surprised and humbled when the pastor asked if they would teach a class themselves. Neither of them has a theological education, and they certainly are no experts in faith matters. The pastor assured them that their task involved facilitating the discussion, helping participants learn from one another, following the resource outline, and learning to explore Scripture together. They attended a two-hour training, and then agreed to teach the class and to host it in their home.

An interesting mix of people signed up for their house group: a thirty-something, new-to-the-church accountant comes with her friend who lives in her apartment complex; a physician and his wife who works at home with Mom duties; a woman who works as a bank vice-president; a younger couple who are both teachers; another dual-career couple with technology backgrounds; and a recently divorced man employed at a sporting goods store.

With everything ready, folks begin to gather, welcoming one another, catching up, getting their snacks, finding their places. An air of comfort has emerged after only a few weeks together and there are handshakes and embraces and good-humored bantering.

Rita opens the meeting with prayer, outlines their time together, and introduces the three parables they will explore from Luke 15. Some have read the Scriptures and the workbook thoroughly, and others have spent less time in preparation, but everyone expresses initial reactions to what they have read. They watch and discuss a ten-minute DVD that corresponds with the workbook, and then Rita moves them through the parables, highlighting key images and offering questions that stimulate discussion. Members have developed a trust that allows intimate reflection. They share easily. While the topic begins with and returns to Scripture repeatedly, the discussion becomes intermixed with stories about friends, news events, personal experiences, concern about relatives. A sense of compassion, an atmosphere of winsomeness, a willingness to listen, and a mysterious and natural intimacy make this time together different from other gatherings, such as staff meetings at work or classrooms at college.

As the evening ends, Joel leads in prayer as people lift concerns: a sister with cancer, a child anxious about school, a youth project at the church, and a controversial election in the community. Afterward, people continue visiting with one another as they leave.

Intentional Faith Development

This scenario describes a typical Bible study that includes some of the key elements that mark a wide variety of small-group gatherings—a focus on faith and Scripture, a sense of community, the sharing of prayer. Some meet on Sunday mornings and others on weekday nights; some studies last six weeks and others continue for decades; some are formal, structured, and driven by lessons and resources while others are freestyle and unstructured. Some groups meet in church classrooms, others in members' living rooms, and others in workplace offices or at schools. Growing together in Christ takes many forms.

Faith development refers to how we purposefully *learn in community* outside of worship in order to deepen our faith and to grow in grace and in the knowledge and love of God. It refers to our active cooperation with the Holy Spirit in our own spiritual growth, a maturation we accomplish through belonging to a faith-forming community such as a Bible study, support group, Sunday school class, house group, women's organization, book study, choir, prayer team, or other small group. Faith development also takes place through retreats, camping ministries, seminars, and support groups that apply faithful living to particular contexts and challenges such as parenting, divorce recovery, living with Alzheimer's, and countless other topics. All of these ministries embed us in a community that helps us to mature in faith and to follow Christ more nearly in our daily living.

By Prearrangement With Myself

How do you find time for Bible study? One young professional woman answered, "By prearrangement with myself. I manage to do other things on time—go to the gym, take children to school and to soccer practice, eat, work. I look at my Bible study as a support group, a regular appointment with God's grace. I make it a priority, as if keeping an appointment with Jesus."

If learning in community fosters faith, why describe the personal practice as *Intentional* Faith Development?

Many followers of Christ desire and value small-group experiences and have benefited from them in the past, but their participation is haphazard, incidental, and infrequent. A short-term study piques their interest at one point and a few years later they attend a home Bible study. Years pass before they go with friends on a weekend retreat. The pattern lacks thoroughness, frequency, and focus. They never practice with enough depth and consistency to feel comfortable or confident with their spirituality. They dabble in religion without growing in grace. Scripture remains strange, mysterious, impenetrable. They enjoy the fellowship but never appreciate close, long-term bonds that lend a sense of trust, strength, and depth to their relationships with others in the community.

Intentional means having a plan in mind. It refers to our determination to act in a specific manner and our having a purpose to what we do. *Intentional* derives from Latin words meaning *to stretch out for, to aim at*. Paul describes this yearning for greater fullness when he writes, "straining forward to what lies ahead, I press on toward the goal for the prize of the heavenly call of God in Christ Jesus" (Philippians 3:13-14). We seek the perfect love of Christ, to have in us the mind that was in Christ Jesus.

Intentional ratchets up the commitment and consistency. Those who practice Intentional Faith Development make room in their lives for learning faith. They *plan* to feed their spirits. Learning faith becomes a way of life, a practice that is no longer haphazard and incidental but which is central and important. They *regularly* participate in Bible studies, seminars, or retreats to focus on cultivating the spiritual life. They desire to know God, and set themselves to the task of learning God's word through Scripture. Learning becomes a lifelong priority, and they seek progressively more challenging experiences to deepen their understanding of God. They feed their curiosity. They desire to mature in Christ and put themselves in the most advantageous situations to do so. Priority, purpose, consistency, persistence, and commitment make faith development *intentional*.

The practice of Intentional Faith Development refers to our purposeful learning in Christian community in order to grow in grace and in the knowledge and love of God.

Jesus Teaches Us to Learn

We learn in community because Jesus taught us to learn this way. He weaved people into a community around him and taught them through stories, parables, examples, and by modeling behaviors. What he taught filtered through the conversations, deliberations, and experiences of his followers as their relationship to Jesus formed them.

The practice of learning in community continued during the beginnings of the early church. The second chapter of Acts reports people gathering in home and temple to learn from the disciples. Before written Scriptures, they repeated the stories of Jesus, imprinting his teachings upon their hearts. The community provided a supportive network for testing ideas, gaining from other people's experiences, sharing the love of Christ, and holding one another accountable to following Christ.

The spiritual life is never a solitary affair.

John Wesley, founder of Methodism, intentionally organized people into small groups for the study of Scripture, prayer, and to "watch after one another in love."[6] Early Methodists met in societies, classes, and bands. They gathered in homes and workplaces and schools. They inquired after one another's spiritual progress with a supportive intimacy. They shared their doubts and hopes and talked about how they had seen God's grace at work in their lives. They learned to "rejoice with those who rejoice" and to "weep with those who weep" (Romans 12:15). They encouraged one another.

Theologically, Wesley based the class meetings on the sanctifying grace of God. *Sanctification* involves our growing in faith and how the Holy Spirit works within us to help us mature in Christ. Faith is not like a light switch, on or off. It is a growth process, as we step-by-step mature in grace intentionally following in the way of Jesus. By the grace of God, we pray that we are closer to God and further along in our following of Christ now than we were five years ago. And we pray that we will be closer to God and further along in our walk with Christ five years from now than we are today.

Sanctification means our faith journey has direction, trajectory, purpose, a path. We desire to become more Christ-like. We grow in grace and in the knowledge and love of God.

According to Wesley, the Holy Spirit makes this maturation process possible. However, growth in Christ requires us to *cooperate* with the Holy Spirit in our own sanctification. We cooperate by placing ourselves in the most advantageous situations for learning God's heart, for walking in Jesus' way, and for remaining faithful in our practice of the spiritual life. A congregation or a community of Christ, such as a Bible study, Sunday school class, or support group, becomes a "school for love" as we learn to give and receive love, to serve others, and to follow Christ more nearly. Community provides the catalyst for growth in Christ.

Solitary Religion Cannot Subsist at All

John Wesley organized followers of Christ "methodically" into small groups—chapels, classes, and bands—so that they would intermix with other people and with the Holy Spirit in their Christian journey. They met weekly to inquire after one another in love. Wesley wrote, "Christianity is essentially a social religion; and . . . to turn it into a solitary one is to destroy it."[7] The spiritual life originates in community and leads to community; we are hard-wired for relationship. In community we discover Christ.

We learn faith in community, not only because Jesus and the New Testament have taught us to learn this way, but also because spirituality cannot be learned alone. Peace, forgiveness, mercy, compassion, hope, gentleness, love, grace, serving—these and many other components of belief and practice are communal in nature. They are social and cannot be learned merely from a book. They become part of us as we practice them with other people. We learn them with friends, teachers, mentors, and fellow travelers on the path with Christ.

And learning in community provides accountability in our walk with Christ. Despite our best intentions and the promises we make to ourselves, our commitment to love God and others often wanes and weakens. When we share the journey with other people, they keep us committed just as we keep them on the path of growth in

Christ. Practices are best honed with the help of others. With fellow followers of Christ comes a sense of accountability that we cannot achieve on our own.

As we follow Christ in the company of other Christians, we implicitly make a public commitment among people we respect and care for and who respect and care for us. Those who share our journey comfort us, provoke us, remind us, sympathize with us, confront us, and pray for us. The Holy Spirit uses them to draw us further along toward Christ.

Work schedules and travel may make regular engagement with community nearly impossible for some people. Supported by community, their faith development takes place mostly in solitude—reading, journaling, searching Scripture, and praying. Even in such circumstances, the Holy Spirit uses other people to prompt and encourage. An entirely solitary religion is an impossible contradiction in the following of Christ.

Growing in Grace

Let's return to Rita and Joel and their Bible study. Look around the living room. An accountant and her friend, two young couples, a bank executive, a doctor and his wife, a divorcé. The reading of Scripture. Workbooks. A short video. Ninety minutes together. Conversation. Prayer. How does the Holy Spirit use these ordinary ingredients to resculpt lives in such extraordinary ways?

An interesting dynamic takes place when we read Scripture and talk about it together with others. Several things happen.

Perspective

Focus on Scripture has the effect of pulling each person out of his or her immediate situation to give a larger view, a slightly more universal perspective. Even if people do not speak aloud about what they are thinking, a topic such as suffering, fairness, jealousy, forgiveness, peace, patience, or sacrifice inevitably draws each toward a personal experience which they are currently facing. The banker listens and mulls over a personnel issue that causes her stress. The divorcé hears the same conversation and reads the same Scripture, but replays in his mind a conversation with his daughter from the night before. The doctor thinks about the estrangement he feels from his sister; one of the young couples casts a knowing glance at each other as they think of the argument they had earlier in the evening. The Spirit moves where it chooses (John 3:8), and its gentle breeze rustles through the souls of each member of the group.

Amazingly, people from vastly different circumstances can read a parable prayerfully, or hear someone share a personal experience about God's activity, and each feels that the topic strikes the target to address a particular challenge in his or her own life.

We Need a Nudge

Tammy said, "Each time I leave a Bible study session, I feel encouraged to do things I was fearful to do before. We always end up talking each other into things—to speak up at work, to forgive a sister, to visit someone who is grieving. We know these are the right things to do. But we need a nudge." Community fosters accountability. We become the voice of Christ to each other.

The benefit of sifting through Scripture with companions is not merely the acquisition of historical facts, theological theories, or ideas. The benefit cannot be reduced to gleaning helpful hints for living or from the advice our friends give us. Each person learns something relevant to his or her soul's desire. Like standing on a balcony looking down from above at all our interactions with others, each person receives a wider perspective on the world in which they work, love, play, and serve. As meaning is unlocked by one person on a topic, an overflowing of insight connects to other persons at an interior level beyond conscious awareness. What we learn may be inexpressible with complete awareness. The Spirit of God works through the conversation, weaving, binding, penetrating, healing, provoking, correcting, reminding, reconciling.

And by the grace of God, with frequent and consistent participation in the faith community, various spiritually sustaining attributes are deepened, and people find themselves with more courage, more patience, a greater compassion, a deeper sense of fairness, a higher commitment to fidelity, more resolve, more peace. The transformation may be gradual, but it is significant and life-changing. Like a potter forming clay, God gently and persistently shapes us.

The fruit of Intentional Faith Development is not merely to know more *about* God but *to know* God, to see through the *idea* of God to God himself. Spiritual knowledge arises in us in mysterious ways. A memorable insight is mulled over and replayed dozens of times during the week that follows a Bible study. We think of it as we wait at the stoplight on the way to the grocery store, it comes to mind as we ride the subway to work, it surfaces during a staff meeting at the office or during dinner with family. Spiritual knowledge is not information we apply to a problem that provides the solution; it's not like a number we plug into a formula that solves everything. Rather, a new awareness takes root; a new perception is formed; a new confidence is discovered; a new connection made; or a new hope recovered that changes how we think, feel, and act. The impact is real, and with the continued practice of spiritual exploration, we experience an increasing benefit, a greater openness to grace, a more refined shaping of ourselves by God. We begin to know God more intimately.

Knowing God, with time, mysteriously causes us to become a different kind of person, with more depth, peace, and courage. We become more hopeful, more thankful, less reactive, gentler, more patient, more resilient, less angry, better able to relate. Sometimes the differences are nuanced and the progress feels imperceptibly slow, like someone taking yoga classes who appears the same from the outside, but who has developed within them a greater flexibility, smoother breathing, and increased circulation. The change is real, but hardly discernable by other people at first. Other times, the change noticeably reshapes outward behaviors. Slow or fast, unrevealed or dramatic—knowing God changes us from the inside out. We follow Christ more closely.

Spiritual Awareness

Focused learning opens the spiritual world to us and stimulates an attentiveness that helps us see elements of soul and grace we might never have noticed before.

Some years ago, I spotted what I thought was an unusually beautiful and rare bird near my home. After searching bird guide books, I discovered that the strikingly colorful bird was actually quite common in my area. After I saw it once, I began to see it regularly. I had long enjoyed an active outdoor life that included camping, hiking, kayaking, and fishing; and I could not believe that I had never noticed this bird before. Spotting this bird permanently changed me. I wondered what else I was missing, and I bought a pair of binoculars, a field guide to birds, and became a birder.

With a new intentionality, I began to read about birds and talk with birders. My eyes and my attitude were now attuned to birds, and with training and experience I began to see them everywhere—unusual birds, striking in their colors and behaviors, were living in my own backyard. I learned where and how to look—on the ground, in the bushes, along the roadsides, under the eaves of buildings. I learned their habits—the shy ones and the boisterous, the flamboyant and the modest. I saw birds I would have overlooked before, noticing them in places I wasn't aware existed. Prior to my "conversion," seeing birds was accidental and unintentional for me; I couldn't discern distinctions, didn't know their names, and had little appreciation for them. Beyond the most ordinary and common, they were unseen and unknown to me. With intentionality, I began to see the world around me from a different perspective, aware of the unseen enchanted world of migration, of nest-building and foraging. I now love birds, and bird books line my shelves and bird drawings adorn my walls. My eyes have been opened to a whole new world.

In the same way, when we open Scripture, belong to a community of Christ, and start to explore life with God, we detect God's presence and activity that we never before noticed. A new world opens. We learn a new vocabulary. With soul work, an unseen world that we never knew existed becomes visible. Regular Bible study with others brings topics before us that we otherwise overlook, and we learn to identify them with greater clarity. We learn to see God.

Jesus came to open the eyes of the blind (Luke 4:18). As we delve into Scripture, we look afresh at our family life, our work world, our inner life, and the world around us. When we notice how the

Spirit moves, we perceive signs of grace. We identify inner attitudes, emotions, and experiences that inhibit growth and happiness—envy, pride, guilt, anger. Hope, joy, forgiveness, service, spirit, grace—these and other elements of faith become visible and tangible. Questions that previously seemed elusive or unimportant become real: How have I experienced God in the past week? How has God sustained me, reminded me, or called me? How is God at work in my life?

Without intentionally cultivating faith, we go through life self-blinded, seeing only a portion of what is before us. We perceive the world through cultural filters that make it nearly impossible to see what is really most important. Whole worlds exist right before us, including the world of spirit, the God-related life, the presence and work of Christ. Learning in community opens our eyes.

Spiritual Sustenance

Belonging to a learning faith community provides companionship that sustains us through difficult experiences. Nothing is as disheartening as a lonely struggle. Many communities and congregations are too large for people to know others well, and so it's in the intimacy of small groups—classes, Bible studies, choirs, prayer groups—that we learn each others' names, pray for one another, and learn to care for one another. Christian companions become the people God uses to sustain us through the ordinary ups and downs of living, and also through those times of extraordinary darkness and grief.

As we pray for one another, community lifts away what obstructs hope. Belonging tempers grief so that it doesn't break us but heals us and makes us stronger. Interwoven into a community, we discover a place of trust, of safety, of love. We feel connected. And that makes all the difference during times of doubt, suffering, or loss. Communion with one another deepens our communion to God.

"I don't know how I would have made it through these last two years without my friends from church." I've heard that repeated by people recovering from grief or simply navigating the ordinary challenges of life. They describe a healthy interdependence rather than an unhealthy dependence or self-deluded independence; they speak of lives interwoven by the grace of God. They describe the benefit of belonging.

The thread of life is fragile. A few cells within a healthy body grow erratically and we receive the diagnosis of cancer; a second's misjudgment at an intersection, and a life is lost; a heart that keeps its cadence for decades skips a few beats and we find ourselves in intensive care; a friend loses her baby during pregnancy; an aging parent shows signs of Alzheimer's; violence strikes someone we know. None of us is immune to such devastating experiences for ourselves, our families, or among our friends. Inexpressible suffering barges in at unexpected moments. And everyone balances the more common (yet anguishing) anxieties, setbacks, and losses that challenge our ability to cope—conflict at home, financial loss, trouble with teenagers, struggles with alcohol, feelings of loneliness. No one lives without facing a threatening darkness.

We overestimate our capacity to handle these things all by ourselves, and we underestimate the power of community to help. Belonging to a caring community, we discover a sustenance that does not answer all our questions or end all our challenges, but which keeps us connected, rooted, grounded. When the worst happens, God doesn't promise us an answer; God provides us a relationship. Through sustaining relationships, we discover that God is not aloof from life and disinterested in us. Instead, God gets in the trenches and suffers with us. We are not alone. God is with us. God's presence reaches us through the people who love us. The thread of life is fragile, but the fabric of life is eternal.

Belonging to a supportive community provides an interpretive context that helps us understand our experience with greater clarity and hopefulness. Perhaps we can't stop the progress of cancer, but in Christian community we find a place to go for refuge, strength, peace, meaning, and hope. Stories from Scripture, mutual prayer, and receiving the embrace of others help us move from one place in our soul to another, from despair to hope, from death to life. We more ably integrate our sufferings into a meaningful narrative that helps us get through the day. Belonging deepens hope; love creates trust; prayer lends strength. A threatening darkness becomes a nourishing darkness with patches of sunlight. We develop resilience as our faith helps us assimilate circumstances that result from events we would never choose. No one can survive significant loss well without being part of a community that cares. Sustained by faith, mortality becomes a catalyst for living more joyfully, intensely, and purposefully. In Christ, by love given and love received, we practice death and resurrection, and we rehearse the continuing narrative of God's grace, creation, and new birth. We flourish.

By ourselves, any one of the challenges that beset us can paralyze us, cause us to become stuck, disconnected, dead. When all that lies ahead vanishes from view, an unassailable hopelessness arises. Community pulls us out of ourselves and carries us toward God.

I remember visiting a woman whose husband had died a few months before. Her friends were concerned because she would never leave the house. She sat in her rocking chair in her living room from morning to evening. In front of her rested the urn that contained her husband's ashes. With his death, her life ended. Every day was spent sitting in her chair focusing on her loss. With continued contact, we convinced her to see a doctor. We began to reconnect her to community, to cast threads to re-bind her to friends and neighbors. People reached for her, and slowly she began to respond. She became part of a women's Bible study, and eventually began to help with projects around the church. Slowly she emerged a new person. Some months later, I visited again. The rocking chair now faced a window with a phone beside it. Letters she was addressing for a church project were scattered on the coffee table. The urn rested on a shelf above the fireplace, still present but no longer the focal point of her existence.

This example has become symbolic for me. Jesus confronted the person paralyzed beside the pool for thirty-eight years with the question, "Do you want to be made well?" (John 5:6). In the gloom of grief, depression, loss, and pain, the answer is not simple. Belonging to a faith community helps us to enfold our past into the present and future, to integrate suffering into a coherent understanding of who we are today and what God intends for our future. Community helps us to flow on, and in the flowing on, hope begins to kill the deadness in our souls.

God also uses community to save us from ourselves and the self-destructive choices we make. Some hardships result from our own massive mistakes, painful misjudgments, and harmful behavior. When we face temptations beyond what we can bear, our friends in Christ reinforce our resolve, strengthen our covenants, and remind us of the critical commitments that bind us. Discussing a passage in Scripture about jealousy, hate, lust, pride, or greed may indirectly address temptations and fears that are far too real and risky to share aloud. Mulling over a Scripture's meaning addresses things diagonally rather than head on, and allows us to contemplate significant issues we otherwise avoid. Bringing such soul work into conscious awareness provides us our best chance to reassess and make good decisions.

Acknowledging the power of temptation and sin, naming them, and exploring them fosters a humility that helps us to restrain ourselves or amend destructive impulses. A thin spirituality that is untested and uncorrected by community leads to self-deception; in honest community, we recognize our incredible capacity to delude ourselves. Jesus says, "Where two or three or gathered in my name, I am there among them" (Matthew 18:20). Christ's voice, in our sisters and brothers, brings us back to ourselves, sustains us, and heals us. In the gift of community we discover the power of confession and of forgiveness, and we find the strength to turn around before it is too late, and to change direction even after harm is done. Friends keep us from falling; and when we fall, they pick us up.

Spiritual Encouragement

In community we catch the contagious quality of faith and hope. Gathering stokes the flames of each member of the group. We encourage one another. (*Encourage* literally means *to put courage into, to give heart!*) We become more in Christ because of the influence of friends. We talk one another into things. We take bolder action that we might otherwise avoid. We follow Christ more eagerly.

Tim worked as a financial officer of a mid-sized business. After his first year, he began to feel uneasy within himself about his job.

The One I Feed

From a Native American faith tradition we receive the story of a grandfather telling his grandchild about spiritual struggle and growth. "Inside me there are two wolves who fight each other all the time. One is motivated by peace, gentleness, honesty, justice, and love. The other lives by resentment, bitterness, hate, anger, and violence." "Which one wins?" asks the child. "The one I feed," answers the elder.

This resonates with Paul's admonition to feed the new nature and starve the old (Romans 13:14). Intentional Faith Development feeds the new creation.

The owners skated close to the edge of acceptable ethical practice, and increasingly Tim felt uncomfortable with their style. During this period, every Bible study Tim attended seemed to be about his situation. During prayer time with his friends, he found himself contemplating what he ought to do. His faith community gave him a vocabulary for understanding what was going on inside, and it gave him the courage to finally speak with his wife about his uneasiness and then to seek the counsel of trusted friends. Without his growing familiarity with the interior life, Tim might never have identified the values that he held that conflicted with the corporate culture. He resigned amicably from his job and moved to another company. Later, his previous employers were accused of major ethical violations. "I just knew it was wrong for my soul," Tim says. "I was struggling with something. It was intuitive and internal, but it was real. Without the friends and the Bible study, I would never have acted." Following Christ educates the heart.

Mutual Care

In community we practice caring for one another. We discover what it feels like to be genuinely prayed for, to have others invest themselves in our well-being, to have confidants who care about what happens to us. In the love others show us, we catch a partial and imperfect glimpse of the complete and unconditional love God has for us. Our burdens are not ours to bear entirely on our own. Our lives become intermingled. By sharing Christ, we share life.

Growth results not merely from what we do, but most especially from *what God does*. Opening ourselves to Scripture, praying for one another, and caring for one another are concrete and personal ways God reaches into our lives to work for our well-being. God uses the stories of countless generations recorded in Scripture and the experiences and love of our friends to sculpt our souls. Our participation invites the Holy Spirit to cooperate with us in the perfecting of our love. Talking and praying and laughing and learning create a dynamic that lifts Jesus' teachings off the printed page and puts them into daily practice. The Bible comes alive, a letter from God, the source of assurance, belonging, and invitation. God works through community.

God has hard-wired us for belonging; learning how to give and receive love is an essential element of human existence and the key to flourishing. Community is the way God feeds our spirits. Jesus said, "I am the vine, you are the branches" (John 15:5). As we stay connected to Christ, we thrive; disconnected, we wither. Community is God's way of bringing us Christ.

The Bible, a DVD, a workbook, conversation, prayer, an unusual assortment of people—what comes of it? Christ. Strength. Life. Learning in community is a means of grace, and it changes our lives.

Why the Hesitance?

If Intentional Faith Development provides such rich spiritual benefits, what keeps us from participating? Why do we resist?

People who have never belonged to a Bible study or adult class hesitate because they fear feeling inadequate or embarrassed by their lack of familiarity with Scripture or with religious terms. They don't know what happens in a class or what will be expected of them. What if someone asks them a question they don't know how to answer? Will they be called upon to pray aloud? They don't know what kind of Bible to bring to the class. They wonder whether they will be accepted. Those who are familiar with the rhythm of small-group spiritual exploration forget how intimidating it is for newcomers. It takes courage and a willingness to handle the awkwardness to break into any new learning situation—Bible study, tennis lessons, or knitting classes. Are we willing to experience the feeling of "temporary incompetence" in order to attain a sense of confidence?

And people resist because they don't know the other people who might be present. It's hard to walk into a room of strangers, wondering whether we will get along with them or whether they will accept us. Will someone dominate the conversations or intimidate others? Will people be impatient with us? How will others react if I disagree? People usually find it easier to join a group when they go along with someone they already know so that they have someone to support them and to talk about the experience with afterwards.

With schedules filled up with work and family obligations, many people simply cannot find time to attend a weekly gathering. In fantasy-like fashion, they await the day when something suddenly changes and they finally have time to nourish their spirit. But no one ever *finds* time; they *make* time. They move other important things around in their schedules and they commit. They decide growing in Christ has such significant impact on other aspects of their living that it's worth making the time.

It's Noticeable

Concert musician Ignacy Paderewski tells about how he continues to practice every day, even after years of focused learning. "If I miss one day of practice," he says, "I notice it. If I miss two days, the critics notice it. If I miss three days, the audience notices it."

Neglect our feeding the Spirit for a few days, and we sense the difference. Something feels unsettled. Avoid it for several days, and our family notices. Neglect the spiritual life for too long, and even those who know us from a distance—neighbors and co-workers—begin to notice.

Sometimes people resist participation because they do not believe all the same things that others in the group believe. I belonged to a Bible study once that was led by someone whose theology was radically different from my own. Honestly, I didn't believe much of what I heard the teacher say, and my faith expression differed considerably from others in the group. Nevertheless, many of the insights shared by others deeply touched me and stimulated me to delve deeper in my own reflection. My relationship with God deepened even though I disagreed with many of the teacher's lessons.

And some people resist participation in an ongoing class because they want the fastest, cheapest, and least transformational route to the spiritual life. They think that merely reading a bestselling book, watching a television broadcast, or following a few simple steps will bring them long-lasting happiness. The prospect of sustained practice, learning, growing, and maturing puts them off. They want quick fixes.

God desires a relationship with us. God wants us to experience the riches of God's grace. When we cooperate with God by placing ourselves in Christian community, we make ourselves more able to absorb God's truth. When we remain too busy or too resistant, God's attempts to reach us are like a pencil on glass and we remain unchanged.

The inner world is a source of power and strength, but it needs to be cultivated. We do so through the practice of Intentional Faith Development.

The Practice of Intentional Faith Development

People who practice Intentional Faith Development commit themselves to learning the faith and growing in grace. They overcome excuses, make time, find a learning community that fits their schedule, and commit to it. They delve deeper.

They find a way to learn that fits their own temperament and learning style. They experiment and explore until something works that sustains their spiritual curiosity and growth in Christ. They persist until they find what's right for them. They learn how to learn.

They consciously avoid the temptation to make scriptural exploration abstract and detached from life. They ask, "What is God reminding me of in this message? What is God inviting me to do, challenging me to learn, or calling me to change?" They connect God to life.

They participate less as a consumer of religion and more as a cultivator of the spiritual life. They don't expect all things to be provided for them. They resist being spoon-fed or merely seeking quick tips or instant success. They internalize life with Christ. They cultivate spiritual life.

People who value Intentional Faith Development teach their children to learn about spiritual matters. They enroll them in children's choirs, Sunday school classes, or vacation Bible school. They talk with their children about what they learn. They cultivate a home atmosphere which encourages faith practices and rewards inquisitiveness, curiosity, and exploration of the spiritual life. They share wonder and honor the enchantment and mystery of life. They make their homes a place of affection where God's love is felt and God's grace is named. They teach faith.

They enjoy much laughter and more love. A learning group becomes a place to relax rather than to tense up. Group dynamics are flexible rather than fragile, and people feel free to be themselves. Laughter is part of the music of faith and tears are the soul's release. They laugh with those who laugh and weep with those who weep.

People who practice Intentional Faith Development avail themselves of increasingly more challenging learning opportunities. They ask themselves, "What am I learning now that is different from an earlier age?" They stretch.

Supported by community, they develop faith in solitude by reading, reflection, and prayer. They carve out time to invite the Spirit in. They create an open, attentive, gracious environment where the Spirit doesn't mind showing up.

They need community as much as they need air. They pray for one another, stay in touch, follow-up, express sympathy, and practice compassion. They love people without needing to fully understand them. They rescue one another from the self-absorption that drains something essential from the soul. They love enough to gently correct. They sustain with a word. Care for others heals their own souls.

They've learned that if they don't repeatedly plow the earth, the ground becomes so hard that nothing new can grow and no seeds can take root. In each season they recommit to some form of study or class or retreat. They open themselves anew to insight. They become resilient, adaptable, and malleable rather than fixed, stagnant, and impenetrable.

People who grow in grace realize that if they follow Christ for a thousand years, they will still need to learn as much on the last day as on the first. The sanctifying grace of God never ceases.

Through the practice of Radical Hospitality, we open ourselves to receiving God's love. We say *Yes* to God. Through Passionate Worship, we love God in return, offering our hearts to God to create us anew. Through the practice of Intentional Faith Development, we grow in grace and in the knowledge and love of God. As we delve more deeply into the spiritual life, we cannot help but perceive God calling us to make a positive difference in the lives of people around us, and this takes us to the next practice, Risk-Taking Mission and Service.

Questions for Reflection

- When have you belonged to a Bible study or class that was helpful, sustaining, and spiritually satisfying? What qualities of the experience made it so?

- What keeps you aware of the spiritual dimension in your daily life? How have you learned to see God in fresh ways?

- When was a time when you or a member of your group helped sustain another person during a time of difficulty or grief? What did you learn about yourself through the experience? What did you learn about Christ?

- What are you curious about in the spiritual life? What are you doing to explore faith more deeply?

CHAPTER FOUR

Loving and Serving Others

The Practice of Risk-Taking Mission and Service

Then Jesus went to work on his disciples. . . . "Don't run from suffering; embrace it. Follow me and I'll show you how. Self-help is no help at all. Self-sacrifice is the way, my way, to finding yourself, your true self."
— Matthew 16:24-25, The Message

Why Serve?

"Why would I want to do that?" Brad asked, at the prospect of getting up early on Saturday morning to join others from the church to prepare lunch for the homeless at a soup kitchen. "I've got my own things going on. I need time for myself and my family. And besides, what difference is it going to make, anyway?"

I've heard those questions spoken by others, and to be honest, I wrestle with them myself. They are not questions of planning and time management, but of spirit, focus, and purpose.

We live to ourselves. It is comfortable, safe, and natural to do so. We take care of our own. Instinct. Self-preservation. Love of family. Cocooning. Enjoying the fruits of our labor. These are important, and we don't need unearned guilt for wanting to rest on the weekend.

Each of us has a whole world of private concerns, personal passions, hobbies, entertainments, family responsibilities, and work obligations. The circle in which we live, work, and play is small, but intense, and important. And it is ours. Why give the time or make the effort to reach beyond our world to serve other people? And would it make any real difference, anyway?

Since time immemorial, prophets and religious leaders, philosophers and poets, reformers and civic leaders have taught the importance of helping those in need, and directing our lives outward to make a difference in the world. They remind us to act with kindness, gentleness, and self-control in our everyday lives in the way we regard strangers. They teach us to interrupt our routines and suffer inconvenience to aid those who are in temporary distress, to tend the injured, comfort the bereaved, feed the hungry. They call us to more deliberate efforts to relieve suffering, protect the vulnerable, and respond to the human trauma of natural disasters with compassion and assistance. They prompt us to address social change, to confront unjust systems, to direct resources toward eliminating disease, and to hold purveyors of violence to accountability. A critical key to a life that is rich in purpose and that, in the end, we find satisfying, involves serving other people and making a positive difference in the world around us. But why is that? Why should we serve others? Why help?

This ethical consensus conflicts with other messages and myths that pervade our culture. "Look out for number one." "Love yourself first." "If we all pursue our own self-interests, the collective results help everyone thrive." "Helping people in need feeds dependency and squelches initiative." "It's survival of the fittest." "Taking care of myself, my own family, and my own community comes first." "People are responsible for their own misfortunes." "Trying to help everyone takes us all down, and sinks the lifeboat." "It's not my problem." "One person's efforts make no real difference at all."

These attitudes influence us, even if we seldom articulate them so pointedly. Sometimes we act as if we believe that if we merely focus on our own personal circle—our work, our family, our homes—that the great issues of human suffering do not impact us, and that we have no role or responsibility. To avoid, deny, ignore, or blame others for the causes of suffering helps us live a carefree, less anxious life.

"Most people, given the choice between having a better world, or a better place within the world as it is, would choose the latter." This cynical analysis of the human condition, attributed to Ralph W. Sockman, captures the magnitude of the issue. Our energy naturally goes to making a better place for ourselves.

Society convinces us that this is the best way to care for ourselves and our families.

So, why serve others? Why work for a better world?

First, some people serve others out of a sense of duty, obligation, and responsibility. Helping others is imperative, and they serve others without regard to the personal cost or inconvenience. If the church needs volunteers at the soup kitchen, they show up. If a community agency needs coats for the poor, they dig through their closets and give what they can. When a hurricane devastates coastal homes, they contribute generously. Being part of the church team means they wear the uniform, show up for practice, and offer their best, and some become quite skilled at the tasks of helping others.

Imagine how it would change your life to take Jesus' commands seriously, and to cultivate such trust that when Jesus says "do it," you would respond with complete and utter obedience. Jesus tells us to feed the hungry, clothe the naked, visit the imprisoned, welcome the stranger. Many people take those words at face value, and offer their best and highest, trusting that whether they enjoy the work or not, these are the right things to do. Following the imperatives of Christ becomes a way of life they adopt wholeheartedly. I've known lay prison chaplains, volunteers at homeless shelters, tutors of underprivileged children, directors of medical clinics, and workers with addicts for whom their initial motivation was simple and obvious: "Jesus tells me to do it, and so I do it." Whatever inner spiritual work, personal passion, or satisfaction they enjoy are after-the-fact results of the activity rather than motivations that initially draw them in. Never underestimate the impact of people motivated by duty.

Second, there are those who serve because helping others contributes to the social fabric of human life. Living in this world requires an unspoken social contract that requires me to help you when you need it, trusting that you will help me when I need it. Serving greases the machinery of social interaction and creates a sustainable mutuality that is essential for co-existence. If I care for you and you care for me, then both of us find ourselves cared for.

This motivation surfaces after catastrophes and natural disasters. People imagine their own home flooded, their own house on fire, their own school struck by violence, and they think of how devastating that would be and how deeply helpful the community would become for them. They gather around, and offer their best, even across great distances. However, the more remote the need, the more difficult it is to see the interconnections and the reciprocities that motivate courageous action to help. While I may be able to imagine my home burning down and temporarily depending upon other people, I may not be able to see myself as a homeless addict living on the streets of the inner city, or as a refugee starving in a camp on a foreign desert, and so I may not see the connection between their lives and mine.

Third, some people discover that serving provides immeasurable personal satisfaction for themselves. They like the way it feels to know that the work they have done, a project they have sponsored, or a policy they have supported has truly relieved suffering, or improved the conditions of people in need. As one person says, "I like myself better and I'm happier when I help others in concrete ways." Making a difference enriches our lives, adds an element of enchantment and adventure and satisfaction that other activities cannot match.

The Holy Spirit purifies all of these motivations when we serve others with the right spirit and focus genuinely on meeting human needs in ways that respect recipients and serve the purposes of Christ.

Need-focused service and passion-driven commitment do not necessarily conflict. In *Wishful Thinking*, Frederick Buechner describes God's call to service and ministry as "the place where your deep gladness and the world's deep hunger meet."[8]

Picture a graph-like matrix. Along the left side of the graph are all the deep human needs, sufferings, and challenges that require bold and courageous service. These are the things God needs people to work on.

Along the bottom of the graph are all the particular gifts and passions that characterize our life. These things personally motivate us. Somewhere on the graph, unmet needs intersect with our own personal passions, and that's where we find ourselves offering effective help. That's where we take our place in God's service, making a difference in ways we find satisfying.

If someone responds only to needs for which they have no passion, they work slave-like for purposes that do not compel them.

On the other hand, if they disregard the world's needs, and only do what they want to do, then they risk offering ministry that is irrelevant for God's purposes, and they serve themselves rather than responding to God's call.

Inner Decision

Philosophers ponder the question of why a stranger walking by a burning building and hearing the cry of someone inside would put his life at risk to enter the building to try to save a person he does not know.

Think about this with me. The stranger who responds puts everything on the line in that moment. He places at risk his entire future—seeing his children graduate and grow to adulthood, holding in his hands his own grandchildren, decades of future earnings and support for his family, years of affectionate partnership with his wife, all that he might accomplish at work and in the community for the remainder of his natural life. In a split-second decision to enter the burning building, he puts all this at risk for a person he does not know and without regard as to whether the person deserves it or not, is healthy or sick, lives with riches or in poverty, or whether the person's prospects for the future are positive or negative. Why does he do it? Is he out of touch with reality?

In that critical moment of pure insight and absolute choice, the person *is not out of touch with reality*. In that moment the person *perceives the truest reality* of all, that our lives are interconnected, that our futures are intertwined with one another, and that we are ultimately one. In moments of such revelation, we see so clearly that we are propelled to the highest and truest of responses. If I let you die, I kill something inside myself.

Ultimately people are not isolated egos, separate and self-absorbed, capable only of self-preservation. I do not live in a universe occupied only by myself. We are one; we belong to one body. In theological terms, you belong to me and I belong to you because we both belong to God. You are my sister or brother and I am yours because God gives both of us life and loves us both unconditionally and completely. God's grace laces our lives inextricably together. When I perceive that reality, I can do no other than to try to help you. In the bold, risky, sacrificial action of entering a burning building to aid a stranger, we witness a raw distillation of the impulses toward what is true. We willingly pour ourselves out because no other way ultimately leads to life.

The deeper truth that we see so clearly in dramatic life-and-death events is one we intuitively perceive in our daily lives and non-critical moments, and this leads us to pour out our lives in small ways each day in service to our families, our children, our communities, and even to strangers. A well-lived life that is in touch with reality involves sacrificing ourselves in the daily care of our children, the love of a spouse, the care of a neighbor, and the service to strangers, each day giving parts of ourselves up, and losing our lives for others. Nothing sustains the flourishing of life and spirit like genuinely pouring ourselves into the lives of others. This does not diminish life; it fulfills it. This is love.

On September 11, 2001, the United States experienced unfathomable pain and loss with the deaths of innocent people. In the countless heroic stories of people who sacrificed their lives to save others, the world also perceived a glimpse of the reality of human connection that was sharper and more focused than we usually see. The tragedy provoked a reality check for countless people, causing them to explore profound questions, such as "Who am I? Who is important to me? How am I related to the people around me? What really matters?" In the brokenness, violence, and grief, we also saw more clearly than usual what is sustaining and trustworthy.

An Essential Truth

Hundreds of scriptural stories reveal this essential truth that our lives are interwoven, and that we discover ourselves fully in giving ourselves to others:

Paul writes, "We do not live to ourselves, and we do not die to ourselves. If we live, we live to the Lord, and if we die, we die to the Lord; so then, whether we live or whether we die, we are the Lord's" (Romans 14:7-8).

Jesus said, "Whoever wants to be great must become a servant. . . . That is what the Son of Man has done: He came to serve, not be served—and then to give away his life. . ." (Matthew 20:27-28, *The Message*).

Jesus taught, "For those who want to save their life will lose it, and those who lose their life for my sake, and for the sake of the gospel, will save it" (Mark 8:35).

Scripture suggests that to encounter Jesus Christ face-to-face in the most tangible way, the whole reality he embodies, involves serving another person by relieving suffering through feeding the hungry, clothing the naked, visiting the imprisoned, and welcoming the stranger. "I'm telling the solemn truth: Whenever you did one of these things to someone overlooked or ignored, that was me—you did it to me" (Matthew 25:40, *The Message*).

Serving others does not merely involve helpful activities that make a difference; Christ-like service helps us become the persons God created us to be. It fulfills God's hope and will for us.

Do we really believe that the ultimate revelation of the heart of God is the life, teachings, death, and resurrection of Jesus Christ? Was Jesus *out of touch with reality* when he embraced the lepers, interceded to protect the vulnerable, healed the blind, took the role of a servant and knelt before his disciples to wash their feet, welcomed the children, ate with tax collectors, told stories about a Samaritan assisting a foreigner, and taught his followers to visit the imprisoned? Or was Jesus *in touch with the truest reality* of all? Do we believe Jesus was leading us toward a flourishing life with these practices, or carelessly leading us astray?

Changing the World

"When you change the world of a child, you change the world."
—Anonymous

By serving others, we bear witness that Jesus' reality is true, that fullness is discovered in the giving and not in the taking; that abundance is found in loving rather than in fearing, that happiness comes in opening ourselves rather than by closing ourselves off.

The real you, your true self, is discovered in letting Christ lead you into serving others with compassion. In serving, we mediate the grace of God. The unsolicited, unconditional love of God that we receive flows through us to others. God's purpose permeates us. As God's love runs through us, we see Jesus Christ more clearly; we work with him and he works through us. Serving puts Jesus' love into practice, and the ultimate reality we see in Christ becomes tangible once again, revealed as a force and power in the world. Serving others, we live the truth.

Separateness, suspicion, distance, fear, and estrangement pale when set alongside the generative, creative power of God's Spirit. We are made separate by fear; by grace, our lives are inextricably interwoven. We can serve out of sheer obedience or out of a sense of mutual obligation, or because we find meaning in it. The bottom line remains: in Christ, human suffering requires response.

Ultimately, the practice of compassionate service in Christ's name grows from interior decision, a spiritual reorientation. As our life with God becomes more vibrant, dynamic, and real, we discover that we can choose to stand in a place of love, of hope, and of risk with an outward-focused posture; or we can choose to stand in a place of fear, defensiveness, protection, and self-absorption. Our hearts turn outward toward others and we follow Jesus toward them, or we focus inwardly and away from others and go our own way. The more consciously aware we become of our interior life with God, the better choices we make. Growing closer to God draws us closer to one another.

Sifting through the motivations to serve takes place under a compelling and all-encompassing mandate, the reign of God. Prophets speak of the day when swords are beaten into plowshares, the wolf and lamb flourish together in peaceful coexistence, we no longer learn war, and the earth is full of the knowledge of God (Isaiah 2; 11). They speak of justice rolling down like waters, and righteousness like an ever-flowing stream (Amos 5:24). New Testament poetry teaches of lifting up the lowly and filling the hungry with good things (Luke 1:52-53). Jesus reveals God's intentions to bring good news to the poor, release to the captives, recovery of sight to the blind, and to set free those who are oppressed (Luke 4:18). Jesus offers glimpses of the kingdom of God, visions of unexpected grace, surprising good news, renewed justice, abiding hope, and ever-present signs of new life. God reigns, and God pulls us toward the new creation. God is ahead, and that truth casts light on all things present. The future belongs to God, and to accept this interpretation of life changes how we think and act, lending hope, urgency, will, and courage to our efforts to follow Christ in serving others.

"Your kingdom come; your will be done, on earth as it is in heaven." With this prayer, we offer ourselves afresh to the reign of God. We align toward God's intended future, we lean forward with hope, and we orient ourselves toward an end where all persons flourish, unrestrained by oppression, disease, or violence. We yearn with body, mind, and soul for the world God wills, and we offer ourselves toward the life God is preparing. We discover our calling to serve within the immeasurably vaster frame of God's purpose in reconciling the world to himself. While many and various motivations *push us outward*, the kingdom of God *pulls us forward*, toward the compelling and glorious end of a world infused by God's love.

How we choose makes all the difference. Whom we trust to follow changes everything. What we believe about ultimate reality is pivotal. Meaningful, fruitful service involves the training of the heart. It begins with interior work. The story we choose to tell determines the life we choose to live.

On an impulse, someone contemplating the life and death of Jesus decided to lie down on her back on the grass of an open field with her arms totally stretched out as if on the cross. She remained in that position in a mood of exploring prayer, thinking about how she felt in that position. *Vulnerable.* That was the single word that captured what she was feeling. To follow Jesus Christ involves trusting that a life with greater vulnerability is richer, and that opening ourselves in risky embrace is not irresponsible, but life-giving.

One Person

Poverty, hunger, war, disease, the suffering caused by natural disasters, addiction, racism, abuse, crime, environmental threat, lack of access to education and healthcare—the challenges are overwhelming, intransigent, impenetrable. They are too big and we are too small. What good can one person possibly accomplish? Do the efforts of like-minded people have any impact?

Imagine that Jennifer, a suburban professional woman in her twenties, prayerfully discerns God's call to focus on alleviating hunger, one of the most complex challenges. Can one person make a difference?

Jennifer studies the root causes of hunger, the international policies that lead to shortages or surpluses, the sustainability of agricultural practices, and consumer patterns. She re-examines her own patterns of shopping and eating. If every person consumed as she does, would the situation improve or deteriorate? Every dollar she spends contributes to the solution or to the problem, and this knowledge becomes a tool for conscientious change. As she connects her personal practices to patterns of land use, fairness in trading, and global trends, she's empowered as a consumer. She adopts a lifestyle more conducive to the alleviation of hunger. Change starts with her.

As she feels more competent about issues that affect hunger, her knowledge shapes how she votes. She advocates for better policies with elected representatives. She makes connections to others who share her passion, and her collaboration gives her a stronger voice with decision-makers.

In Jennifer's professional work, she attends to questions about the impact her business practices have on people—on employees, communities, schools and young people, and on the environment. She connects what she has learned about hunger and influences corporate policies and practices in ways that help.

Next, she searches for opportunities to volunteer her time. A local food bank supplies resources to homeless shelters for distribution. Nutrition programs in schools aim at children in poverty, community centers provide lunches for seniors, and Meals-on-Wheels ministries help the homebound. A new world opens up before her in her own community. Jennifer sees hunger first-hand in the eyes of people at an emergency shelter and listens to a mother who has no idea how she will feed her children the next day. She explores the work of the Red Cross and Heifer International. She finally commits to a particular social agency which does excellent work, and that needs her gifts. She feels at home with the other staff and volunteers. She offers her best.

She connects with people who share her passion. She speaks to church groups and teaches classes about hunger. She takes the youth group to visit service agencies. She serves on a congregation-wide initiative to Africa. Her passion for alleviating hunger shapes her financial giving. And she prays daily for those who suffer from hunger as she invites God to show her other ways to make a difference.

Personal lifestyle changes, advocacy, hands-on volunteer service, teaching others, contributing money, prayer—there are hundreds of ways she can make a difference and impact hunger. The options are endless, and her passion fosters as many or as few activities as she has time and energy to fulfill.

Imagine that Jennifer pursues this calling with passion for the remainder of her life. Imagine forty or fifty years of learning, volunteering, leading, and contributing. Imagine that she deepens her knowledge and skill, and works more actively in some phases of life than in others as she balances this calling with work, family, and leisure. The cumulative impact is huge. Jennifer transforms the lives of hundreds of people locally and directly, invites and involves others through church and community, and strengthens agencies that help around the world.

With prayerful imagination, we can think of just as many personal responses to any challenge—abuse, violence, war, addiction, disease, poverty, education, healthcare. Any subcategory—literacy, Alzheimer's, organ donation, single parenting, immigration, alcoholism, depression—provides an array of opportunities by which one person can make a substantial difference. Through disciples following Jesus, God transforms the world.

If everyone thinks that nothing can be done, then nothing will be done. In ways mysterious beyond our comprehension, God multiplies our personal efforts, interweaves them with the work of others, and uses them to transform the world. This is fruitful living.

With the best of intentions, many followers of Christ help with a small project at the church every once in awhile. Service is sporadic, infrequent, and inconsistent. They dabble in doing good. But without focus, consistency, and persistence, we feel frustrated, awkward, and ineffective in serving. We're like students signing up for one tennis lesson, one piano lesson, one dance lesson, one woodworking lesson, and one swimming lesson; when we look back over time, we wonder why we've never mastered any of them. Competence and effectiveness in compassionate service derive from sustained effort through the periods of feeling incompetent and awkward to the stages of practice, repetition, and nuanced learning to the advanced phases of graceful and fruitful expression.

Those who make the biggest difference take the long view. They practice. They learn. They grow in effectiveness. They persist. Like the river that cuts a great canyon through the rocks over millions of years, their effectiveness at changing overwhelming conditions derives from enduring consistent, repeated, focused action.

With the scattering of seeds, a harvest presently unseen comes to fruition. Huge trees thrive where once a few seeds were planted by visionary and committed people. Compassionate service helps us discover a notion of personal mission.

Employed by Thee or Laid Aside for Thee

The Covenant Prayer, composed and adapted by John Wesley, invites complete humility and obedience to God's service, asking God to work through us or to work around us, and to take us to places and put us alongside people we would never choose for ourselves.

"I am no longer my own, but thine.
Put me to what thou wilt, rank me with whom thou wilt.
Put me to doing, put me to suffering.
Let me be employed by thee or laid aside for thee,
exalted for thee or brought low for thee.
Let me be full, let me be empty.
Let me have all things, let me have nothing.
I freely and heartily yield all things
to thy pleasure and disposal. . . ."[9]

With consistent practice, serving becomes integrated into our sense of self, a permanent part of our identity. We experience *a sense of purpose* that runs deep. Living with purpose means our life has a direction toward which we move that draws us forward despite difficulties, setbacks, and detours. Those who make a huge difference live with a palpable *sense of purpose* that is passionate, resilient, imaginative, vibrant, and persevering. It's contagious and inviting. It's as much a part of them as their personality or sense of humor. It becomes them. They become servants. They align with something true.

Nothing in the spiritual life adds so much satisfaction as truly making a positive difference in the lives of others. Serving others helps those we serve flourish; and we flourish in the serving of others.

Training the Heart

"What in the world am I doing here? I can't tell you how many times I've found myself asking that question." That's how Ken tells about the unexpected places his faith journey has taken him. Ken is a medical technician in his mid-fifties, a husband and father, a tennis player, and a handyman. He belongs to a congregation where he has attended worship for more than 25 years. He first helped with the Thanksgiving baskets, gathering canned goods and perishables and delivering boxes to families in need. Then Ken worked with the youth group on a week-long housing rehab project.

Later Ken received training and led a work team to Nicaragua where they rebuilt a school damaged by a hurricane, and they taught children. Now he mentors new members who want to get involved with hands-on service projects. "I never imagined myself doing this," he says. "But it answers the question, *What in the world am I doing here?* This is the reason God put me here."

Ken followed a path that fit his gifts, context, and passions. Other peoples' pathways differ dramatically, and yet they follow a similar trajectory. Followers say *Yes* and help in small ways with a project. They catch the spirit, noticing the difference their work makes for others and for themselves. They mature and gain confidence, branch out or deepen their commitment, and with time and a pattern of consistent service, they end up somewhere totally unexpected. Their own inner maturing in Christ makes a difference in the lives of other people and transforms the world.

Shirley's volunteer stint for a women's shelter led to repeated patterns of helping that opened the door for her work on their board of directors. This fed other passions she had, and she used her board-acquired skills to support literacy for children, which led her to teach volunteers at a literacy center, which has led to her involvement in school district educational initiatives.

Ana's volunteer teaching of elementary classes for Sunday school and vacation Bible school led to her helping with a week-long VBS program in cooperation with an inner city church that reaches out to families with single moms. She loved it, and formed relationships with the moms that led to her volunteer work in a jobs training program and the establishment of an urban child-care program to support working single moms.

After Lance's retirement, he helped with a "clean up day" around the church with other retirees. He enjoys working outdoors with his hands, and he saw the need for more consistent care and repair of the church facilities. He and a friend worked together twice a month, trimming trees, planting bushes, painting doors, fixing leaks. He was invited to serve on the Grounds Committee. Lance was asked his opinion about the grounds at the community cemetery that had fallen into disrepair. Now he tends the cemetery, recruiting other retirees to help.

Ruth was in her late seventies when her husband died and she fell into a severe depression. The pastor encouraged her to visit her doctor and invited her to volunteer in the church office. She redis-covered long-neglected skills she had developed as an office worker decades before, and organized tasks in ways that helped the church. She became the support person for the mission volun-teers who rebuild houses, feed the homeless, and visit shut-ins.

Earl was new to the faith when he attended a *Walk to Emmaus* retreat. He experienced a powerful personal transformation that led him to volunteer with future retreats. After two years of sup-porting and leading *Emmaus*, he felt called to help with *Kairos* prison-based retreats. He served on a planning team and then spent a weekend locked down with inmates to offer the retreat for them. He became active both with victims' rights organizations and prison reform agencies.

Jan has a career that takes her on the road constantly. With more than a hundred flights each year, her job does not allow her to embed herself into the community the way Ruth has, or to commit to regular volunteer service as Shirley does. How could she prac-tice compassionate service? That was on her mind as she visited with the director of a hospice program that had helped her aunt during her terminal illness. Jan offered suggestions to improve the program's website and communications. Eventually, she served as an advisor to the director, regularly exchanging ideas by email and phone. One patient particularly touched her, and with the family's permission, she made contact by phone. This became her pattern, phoning daily to check in, listen, encourage, and pray. If you want to serve, a way opens.

Sondra occasionally used her nursing skills to support weekend projects at her urban church that has an active ministry for the homeless, for addicts, and for people living with HIV. She served food at the shelter, distributed clothes, and assisted people in locating housing. She also raised money for her congregation's partner church in Mozambique. When she visited Mozambique, the experience changed her life. African American herself, she became passionate about health issues in Africa, raising funds for malaria nets, organizing medical teams to work in Africa, and working as an advocate on world health issues and the diseases of poverty. She has spoken to dozens of churches and helped other people serve the poorest of the poor.

What in the world am I doing here? One thing leads to another and leads to another. With a disciplined pattern of serving and of opening themselves afresh to following Christ, all of these persons have ended up somewhere they could never have imagined. They each make a real difference in the lives of others, and they are changing the part of the world God has given them to transform.

Risk-Taking Mission and Service changes the lives of those who offer ministry. It changes the lives of those who receive ministry. It changes the world as we share directly with God in the creating and re-creating work that makes all things new.

Start anywhere and at any time. It is never too late. And with continued cultivation and with the passage of time, the difference we make multiplies and the sense of satisfaction we experience deepens. When we answer Jesus' call, "Follow me," there's no predicting where we will end up!

Each person's work is like a seed, taking root, sprouting, breaking the surface, branching out, blossoming, and eventually casting other seeds to other places and becoming fruitful in ways beyond measure. Such stories are repeated in congregations and communities throughout the world. A follower responds to an invitation, a response made possible by the interior work that prepares them to act boldly. With continued practice they experience an internal shift in priorities, subtle redirections of effort, slight corrections of course that help them find the right place and right work that God calls them to fulfill. Their personal passions and strengths become relevant for addressing human need. Serving involves trusting Christ, and taking the next step, and the next, one after another.

Such fruitfulness may appear unachievable. Many of these stories took ten or twenty years to unfold. Incremental steps, persistence, passion, and time take us from here to there.

We may look at these examples with a guilty sense of repugnance. We may not admit it, but we don't even *want to want to* do some of these ministries—hospice care, soup kitchens, Third World countries. But these examples do not describe *your* path; you may be called to make a difference in an entirely different way. These are not prescribed paths; rather they stimulate our thinking and discernment. Many of these people felt the same way when they began. Their tastes, interests, desires, and tolerances have adapted from the beginning of their journeys until now. They didn't start by wanting these outcomes for themselves. They embrace situations now that they would have avoided at an earlier time, and they are now mystified by their former disgust. That's typical of God's calling.

Risk-Taking: Overcoming Fear With Love

Service refers to the volunteer impulse animated by the Spirit of God that causes people to offer their time, energy, and leadership to help their congregations and communities thrive. Through service, we become "doers of the word, and not merely hearers" (James 1:22), putting our faith into practice in concrete and visible ways. The church fulfills its mission through the active, altruistic, generous offering of mind, muscle, and spirit by people who sing in choirs, chair committees, manage rummage sales, assist with ushering, visit homebound members, coach soccer, paint the classrooms, and greet visitors. Service strengthens congregations and changes the lives of those who offer it.

Mission turns service outward and focuses beyond the walls of the congregation. Mission extends God's love to the people of the community, the nation, and the world, and refers to the positive difference we make in the lives of others, whether or not they will ever become part of the community of faith. Mission involves our deliberate effort to improve the conditions of others; to relieve suffering; confront injustice; heal disease; and assist during times of crisis, loss, or grief. Mission pulls us out of ourselves and connects us with people we don't know. Service and mission are grace-driven, propelled by God's love for all people.

Jesus pushes us to extend our empathy to those not already in our circle of concern, and invites us to inspire others to do the same. "Here is a simple rule of thumb for your behavior: Ask yourself what you want people to do for you; then grab the initiative and do it for them! If you only love the lovable, do you expect a pat on the back? . . . Help and give without expecting a return. You'll never—I promise—regret it" (Luke 6:31-36, *The Message*).

An outward-focused life flows naturally and inescapably from following Christ, and early followers visited the sick and the imprisoned, provided resources for the poor and vulnerable, reached out to people in need and drew them in by the grace of God. An initiating and active grace put love into action, and bore witness to the world of the living Christ. To live "in Christ" means not only are we sustained by the presence of God's love revealed in Christ, but that the Spirit of Christ permeates us and motivates us to serve. "In Christ" means our identity derives from full-bodied openness to Jesus' way. Our faith in Christ proves its relevance in how we treat others.

If these vigorous practices represent mission and service, why modify the expectation with *Risk-Taking*?

The practice of *Risk-Taking* Mission and Service pushes us out of our comfort zone and into places we would never go on our own. Those who practice Risk-Taking Mission and Service place themselves in situations that will change their minds. They voluntarily set aside their own convenience for a higher purpose. They follow Jesus into areas they would not tread on their own volition. They practice service with passion and intentionality, pouring themselves out for others. They go where Jesus leads, even when it is uncomfortable, awkward, unexpected, and costly. They risk.

A Teacher's Lesson

One rainy night I started up the stairwell to my seminary apartment when I encountered one of my theology professors. Dr. D. was one of the most respected theologians of his generation, and I was completely surprised to see him in a student dorm. Dressed in his suit and tie from his day's teaching and covered by a wet overcoat, he was carrying bags of groceries up the stairs. I offered to help, and as we walked together I heard the story. The wife of a student had become gravely ill and was undergoing cancer treatment. They had been much in our prayers. Dr. D. had visited with them, and offered to help in any way he could. As a result, he went shopping for them after he finished his classes. He'd been doing this for weeks. Nothing I learned from him in the courses he taught had as much personal impact on me as finding him in that staircase on a cold, rainy night.

At the moment we face human suffering, a choice presents itself. If we pay careful attention to our natural tendencies, we discover that we desire to move away. We want to avoid pain, to deny the problem, to turn the other way. We are pulled toward safety. Fear and anxiety move us to secure and predictable territory.

If we listen deep within our soul, we discover that something inside us also draws us *toward* the suffering. Every human soul that harbors the tendency to avoid suffering also houses the capacity to respond compassionately. One path compels us away from pain; the other evokes the desire to help.

If we move toward suffering rather than running from it, we experience uncomfortable moments and awkward incidents. We risk feeling helpless, or worse, we risk sharing the pain of the person who suffers. Opening ourselves is listening to someone share their loss without changing the subject; walking into a nursing home full of elderly patients and remaining there long enough to show that someone still cares; listening to people of different races tell us we will never be able to understand them; standing alongside people in their struggles to overcome, rebuild, and heal. It leaves us vulnerable.

God's call moves Jesus' disciples toward people in distress. In the Letter of James, we find, "Religion that is pure and undefiled . . . is this: to care for orphans and widows in their distress" (James 1:27). Visiting the sick, the suffering, the unjustly treated, and the lost is not possible if we follow our own inclinations, living by fear rather than by love.

At the crucial moment in our encounter with suffering (*crucial moment* literally means "the moment of the cross") when we decide whether to move away or toward it, following Jesus inevitably moves us toward people. Turning toward suffering is a moment of grace, the gift-like initiating love of God streams through us. Love defeats fear, life overcomes death, compassion stands victorious over estrangement. When we reach toward another, a new birth takes place, the creative dynamic of the Holy Spirit binds us together.

Training the heart to follow Christ involves learning to overcome fear. We acknowledge it and understand it, but choose to live by love instead. As we feed the impulses to act with love by consistent practice, we find courage to do things we would not otherwise do. Practices bring overwhelming tasks into manageable scope, reducing unreachable challenges to a size that is embraceable and doable. Practices involve steps that we take with consistency and frequency that lead us where we need to go. No one can face world hunger with confidence. But we can serve at the soup kitchen twice a month, write a congressional representative twice a year, and contribute to a reputable charity annually. We decide that the deliberate action is worth the effort.

Many times we know the right thing to do, but where can we find the courage to act? Our relationship with God and the community of Christ fosters confidence and hope. Risk-Taking Mission and Service are where courage and joy intermingle.

God's Spirit turns dentists into team leaders for Habitat for Humanity, school teachers into clinic hosts, store clerks into language tutors, accountants into Big Brothers, stay-at-home mothers into lobbyists for legislation that protects the uninsured, college professors into volunteer prison chaplains, car salesmen into cooks for mission teams, retired folks into literacy tutors, and can change you into something you can't now imagine.

Are you willing to put yourself in a situation that may cause you to change your mind?

Social Change

Feeding one person at a time, visiting one prisoner at a time, and building one house at a time are vitally important. Hands-on, face-to-face ministry changes lives. The grace of God flows from person to person through life-changing mission. However, people who practice Risk-Taking Mission and Service also discern God's call to involve themselves in social change, political activity, and community causes. Some people offer themselves to change systems, confront injustice, and relieve suffering on a larger scale. The tools for change become policies, funding initiatives, and petitions rather than hammers, cooking pans, and wheelchair ramps. The imperative of God's love propels people into the struggle for change at all levels—personal, family, congregational, community, national, and global.

John Wesley's *inner holiness*, the sanctifying and perfecting love at work inside us, finds outward expression in *social witness*, a dedicated commitment to changing conditions that rob people of fullness of life. Social witness serves God, who is the "lover of justice" (Psalm 99:4). To have in us the mind that is in Christ means we perceive God's activity not merely in stories of personal transformation but in the great shifts of history toward justice, release from oppression, and relief from suffering.

"Justice is love with legs," one seminary professor said. God's love takes a social form, a political expression, when the followers of Jesus learn to love strangers by relieving suffering through programs that prevent diseases, healthcare systems that serve all people, and labor policies that are fair. Social justice ministries seek the conversion of social structures toward greater justice, helping people to flourish.

Victims of violence, poverty, discrimination, and people who suffer through war, famine, or natural disaster often lack the power to effect change that will relieve them or transform their circumstance. If no one with power and resources speaks for them or stands with them, how can their voices be heard? To *advocate* means to speak for, to act on behalf of, to give support. Among the most important ways followers of Christ express God's gracious love is through advocacy, speaking for the children, the oppressed,

"I Never Would Have Chosen This for Myself"

Frank was an active church member in the 1960s when his daughter was arrested for drug possession in a foreign country. Her arrest happened at a critical time in the country's internal politics. They made an example of her, and she was unexpectedly sentenced to years of hard labor. Thus began Frank's several-year saga of personal pleadings, meetings with diplomats and policy-makers, and exposure to the extreme conditions of prison systems. He found support from his community of faith and the teachings of Scripture. The witness of Amnesty International motivated him to continue his service and advocacy long after his own daughter's release. For more than thirty years he directed his energies to creating more humane criminal justice systems, establishing treaties to eliminate torture and to abolish the death penalty. "I never would have chosen this for myself," he says, "but given what happened to my family, I felt called to do all I could." Victims become survivors by discovering the inner calling of God to turn their personal suffering into channels for connecting with others for the transformation of the world.

the homeless, the poor, and the marginalized who cannot speak for themselves.

As followers of Jesus, we look at the world through the perspective of someone who suffered innocently—a person who was crushed and broken by the world's powers—rather than through the lens of privilege, power, and wealth. Christianity began with catastrophic brokenness and violence, resulting in a persevering, sacrificial love that drives us to work on behalf of the suffering with unending passion. We can do no other. To follow Jesus in first-century Palestine meant walking into the caves of lepers, confronting violence against women, embracing children, exposing self-serving judges, condemning money changers, and challenging the indifference of the wealthy toward the poor and vulnerable. To follow Jesus today involves walking into HIV clinics, confronting abuse of power by government officials, challenging corporate greed and unfair labor practices, praying for peace, and supporting healthcare for children.

Social change is risky. Some social witness the world understands—seeking cures to cancer, protecting children from abuse, supporting victims of violence. Other forms of social witness the world cannot fathom because the ideas run counter to deep cultural biases or because such initiatives seem foolish, unrealistic, or hopeless—working with violent offenders, protesting torture, establishing programs for drug addicts, organizing for peace, protecting the rights of immigrants. Public opinion stoked by moral conviction can leverage powerful change.

Most of the people reading this book are the beneficiaries of various forms of privilege. Most of us have enjoyed opportunities to make a living; live freely; feel protected by the law; and benefit from medical, financial, and educational institutions. Most of us have probably made conscientious choices based on good motives. We do our best.

Yet some of the benefits we enjoy have derived from belonging to systems that hurt the planet, take advantage of the poor, or depend upon oppressive labor practices in foreign countries. Some of the opportunities we have enjoyed were closed to others for no reasons other than race, nationality, or financial advantage. People can live personally responsible and moral lives while also unknowingly or unwillingly participating in systems that are immoral or hurtful.

Prophetic voices help us see the incongruity between what we believe and the personal choices we actually make. The dissonance is uncomfortable. We want such voices to be wrong, even when we intuitively know that some of what they say is true. Listening attentively rather than reacting with indignation may cause us to rethink and to act with greater fairness and more compassion. Then we are able to influence systems and make personal choices that align more truly to the deep principles we hold. God speaks to us sometimes through the voices of people who disagree with us and who really irritate us just as the prophets of the Old Testament bothered the comfortable, complacent, wealthy, and powerful in days gone by. They rally us to a necessary collective sense of responsibility.

Part of the hard inner work of perceiving God's activity involves developing a social consciousness, a heightened awareness of how our lives interconnect with others in positive as well as hurtful ways. Belonging to a community, working for a company, or enjoying the benefits of citizenship involves taking responsibility for their directions, policies, and practices. How can we do less harm and more good? *How do we have in us the mind that is in Christ Jesus?* is a social question as well as a personal one.

In following Christ, one of the greatest risks is the sin of omission, failing to do the things we ought to do. Sometimes we know what is right, but a lack of courage or a failure of nerve makes us afraid to act. Our self-interest and unwillingness to act are offensive to God. With any social justice initiative, people will disagree, resist, and push back. Conscientious people we love and respect will disagree with us. Effective work requires humility, grounding in Christ, a willingness to listen and to learn, and a positive perseverance.

People are hungry for what makes a positive difference. Some find their place in personal, hands-on, face-to-face contact. Others find themselves called by God to offer themselves as change agents at the public, corporate, or policy level. Both deserve our prayerful support and discernment. We are personal disciples and social creatures, and God's grace leads us to private action and public change. God forms us in the way of Christ for the transformation of the world.

Famine is real. Disease is real. Devastating birth defects caused by toxins in the environment are real. Killing is real. Addiction, desperation, violence, and poverty are real.

In a world where these things are real, what kind of person do you want to be? What kind of person do you think God wants you to be?

The Practice of Risk-Taking Mission and Service

People who practice Risk-Taking Mission and Service understand obedience to Christ. Some things they do, not because they enjoy it, but because Jesus Christ would do it, invites them to do it, or commands them to do it. They go where Jesus goes.

They improve on how to have a greater impact. They become progressively more strategic in their service, learning to maximize effectiveness and fruitfulness. They learn to serve.

Whether their service involves bricks and mortar, soup kitchen lunches or blanket distribution, money-raising or legislative initiative, they consciously focus on the people being served. They treat people with dignity. They see the face of Christ in those they serve, and they represent the grace of God in their serving. They do not patronize.

They saturate their work with prayer, finding strength, grounding, motivation, and calling in their relationship with God. Through serving, they discover God; through God, they discover serving.

They do not think more highly of themselves than they ought to think. They practice humility. The difference they make comes from God.

They live their spiritual convictions, examining whether what they do in their employment is consistent with their desire to serve God and others. They avoid harmful practices that take advantage of the poor or which further violence or damage the earth. They strive to eliminate prejudices such as those related to race, religion, gender, nationality, age, or economic condition from their own lives and workplaces. They promote justice, and their lives give testimony to the fair treatment of people and a concern for the disadvantaged. They practice God's new creation.

They treat well those whom society seems to think it's all right to mistreat—maids, waiters, cash register attendants, ticket counter people, store shelvers, custodians, street vendors, people of other nationalities, groundskeepers, and others in the service industry. Serving Christ is not merely about major projects and coordinated work teams, but about one-on-one, person-to-person respect, courtesy, and helpfulness. They listen. They notice people whom others overlook. They express appreciation. They treat people the way they would want to be treated.

People who serve in the Spirit of Christ do not demean or dismiss people by ignoring them. They serve expecting nothing in return, and they do not offer gifts that impose a burden or dependency. Their service doesn't exact a cost in dignity from those who receive.

The World God Has Given You

Mr. Martinez is in his eighties and has been a follower of
Christ for more than sixty years. He is nearly blind and has a
hard time getting around on his own. Twice each week his
daughter drives him to a retirement home where he visits and
cares for six fellow church members. Some of them are long-
time friends, and others were identified by the pastor as needing support. He reads the paper with them, helps them with
their mail, brings them books, watches baseball with them,
and prays for them. He provides a rich ministry. He takes it
seriously, and it makes a huge difference. The part of the world
God has given Mr. Martinez to transform is a single retirement
center.

God uses the church to make disciples of Jesus Christ for
the transformation of the world. What portion of the world has
God given you to transform?

They never regard people as objects, things, or statistics. When
they serve on medical and construction teams, they do not treat
people as soulless bodies. When they serve on worship, teaching,
and pastoral care teams, they do not treat people as bodiless souls.

They *practice* serving. Serving is something learned, and there
are no instant experts. They begin small, anticipate feelings of temporary incompetence, and they build up their "serving muscles."
They practice when it's easier not to; they overcome internal resistances and external criticism; they serve when they feel awkward
and clumsy doing it; they do it with others and learn from mentors;
they never stop serving until they feel confident, graceful, and natural doing it. They become servants.

Those who practice Risk-Taking Mission and Service take the
long view, knowing that the conditions that cause suffering—
poverty, disease, violence, hunger—do not arise overnight and
they are not solved quickly. They do not lose hope. They never give
up. They persist.

They approach the suffering of other people with both awe and
joy. They walk gently with those who are vulnerable.

They expand boundaries to get the job done. They work with other churches, other denominations, non-church and governmental agencies, and businesses to help people in need. The work of the Holy Spirit is not confined to those who call it by that name. They collaborate.

People who serve Christ by serving others don't go it alone. They immerse themselves in community. They've inherited their ministry from others and will pass it along to others; they balance one another's weaknesses and strengths. They do not insist on their own way. They submit willingly to the wisdom of the body of Christ.

They do not avoid the hard tasks, the unsolvable problems, the persistent challenges.

They are more interested in impacting lives in positive ways than in receiving credit. They easily express appreciation to others and give thanks to God.

They accept the uncertainty of outcomes. When addicts return to their drugs, newly constructed houses are flooded again, scholarship recipients drop out of school, or parolees steal from the soup kitchen, they persevere. They scatter more seeds.

They mature from "what's in it for me?" to "how can I help?" and from "they ought" to "I will."

They find a way. Nobody is too far away, no village too remote, no obstacles too large, no resistance too severe that they can't figure out some way to make a positive difference. They connect, collaborate, negotiate, think, plan, borrow, strategize, and push until a way opens.

They take hardship, resistance, setback, and disappointment in stride, knowing that if serving people was always easy, fun, and convenient, then it wouldn't have taken Christ to teach us, and he wouldn't have told us about taking up crosses.

They invite young people to serve alongside them, share their experiences with children, and teach the next generation how to serve. They turn over the reins of leadership when the time is ripe.

They mobilize others to meet human needs. They inspire and lead and teach. They do not coerce or use guilt. They invite and support. They help people take first steps.

People who serve in Christ's name evaluate projects in order to improve their ministries so that they become more fruitful. They invite feedback. They do better with each project. They excel in doing good.

They honor service in many forms—hands-on, policy-oriented, social activism, service on boards, personal engagement, charitable donation. They respect those who are out front as well as those who work behind the scenes.

They don't merely pray for peace; they work for it.

Grounded in Grace

Through the practice of *Radical Hospitality* we open our lives to God's initiating love and invite God into our hearts. We say *Yes* to God's grace.

Passionate Worship connects us to God and fosters our love for God; the things that matter to God begin to matter more to us. God reshapes our hearts and minds.

Intentional Faith Development deepens and matures our relationship with God as we learn God's Word and practice it in community. We perceive God's calling with greater clarity as we explore the inner landscape of soul and spirit. We grow in grace and in the knowledge and love of God.

Growing in Christ, we cannot help but feel called to make a positive difference in the lives of others, and so we offer ourselves in Christ-like service. God loves the poor and outcast; suffering breaks God's heart. *Risk-Taking Mission and Service* stirs in us a sense of enchantment about the larger world, and through this practice we experience the mystery of another person's life in ways that add depth to our own. God pushes us out of our comfort zone. We love those whom God loves. We offer God's hope. Our discipleship and following of Christ begins to transform the world around us.

Each step is grace-driven. Each practice trains the heart. God's love insinuates itself deeper into our souls, drawing us toward a life rich in what matters most: faith, hope, and love.

At some point, we realize that all that we have and all that we are belong to God. And that leads us to the practice of *Extravagant Generosity*.

Questions for Reflection

- Who taught you to value serving others? How did you learn to serve? Who modeled the life of service for you? What's your earliest memory of helping others as an expression of your faith?

- What motivates you to serve, to relieve suffering, or to seek justice? Do you delight in doing good?

- What particular gifts, abilities, or experiences prepare you to make a positive difference personally? In your community? In the world?

- Where have you seen God at work in the midst of loss and suffering? How have you been a part of God's work?

- When have you moved out of your "comfort zone" in order to help another person? What has been "risk-taking" about your service to Christ?

- What do you consider the three most critical issues that require response and service to improve the human condition and relieve suffering? Where do you see yourself fitting in and making a difference?

CHAPTER FIVE

The Grace of Giving

The Practice of Extravagant Generosity

"This most generous God who gives seed to the farmer that becomes bread for your meals is more than extravagant with you. He gives you something you can then give away, which grows into full-formed lives, robust in God, wealthy in every way, so that you can be generous in every way. . . ."
—*2 Corinthians 9:11,* The Message

Giving helps us become what God wants us to be.

As a pastor, each year I preached on tithing and proportional giving in preparation for Consecration Sunday, the day members offer their annual pledges to support the church's ministry.

Before the service one year, Terri and Charles visited me in my office. Terri described what happened the previous year during the preparation for Consecration Sunday. In my sermon I said that giving is not merely about the church's need for money, but about the Christian's need to give. Afterward, she and Charles had a long, difficult conversation about the sermon. She poured out her heart about her unhappiness with the way they were living, and Charles agreed. "We couldn't breathe," she said. "We were living a lie. We had a big beautiful house, two cars, a boat, and everyone thought we were so happy. But underneath we were stressed out, arguing all the time about money, in debt over our heads, and we felt miserable. We were strangling."

Terri and Charles both had high-income, professional careers. They earned plenty. "But we lived in constant fear," Terri said. "We were afraid of what others would think if we downsized our house or traded in our cars or stopped doing the things everyone else was doing. We were afraid of the bills, the debts, the banks. We were scared of what would happen if one of us became sick. We were afraid of the shame of bankruptcy. We were afraid our teenagers would find out how precarious our situation was. And we didn't talk about it for fear our marriage couldn't withstand the stress."

Terri was now wiping tears from her eyes as she continued the story. Last year, after the sermon, they had talked honestly about all of this for the first time, and Terri had courageously said to Charles, "What kind of life does God really want us to have? Not this kind!"

Thus began the journey a year before that had brought them to my office that day. They finally faced what they had been avoiding. With prayer and courage, they had filled out last year's pledge card giving one percent of their expected income. When they offered it up to God, they sealed it with a commitment to start fresh in all things related to money. They read books, took a course, and consulted a professional. They spoke with their children and included them in a plan to turn their lives around. Some decisions were major—to move into a more modest neighborhood and to sell a high-payment car in order to buy a used one. They cancelled credit cards. Like a team on a mission, the family dialed back expenses. They ate at home, repaired things themselves, and planned a modest vacation. They spent more time talking together as a family. They adopted a plan and adapted their lifestyle to live comfortably while paying off debt, saving money, and giving more. Charles said, "A year ago, we never imagined that we would feel the peace we feel today. It seemed totally beyond reach."

After finishing their story, Charles pulled from his pocket their pledge card for the upcoming Consecration Sunday, handed it to me, and said, "Pastor, it's not huge, but it represents two percent of our income for this next year. Our whole family is committed to watching that number grow year by year. All of us have signed the card, and when we offer it we will renew our commitment to God and to each other as a family. Giving has become a gift to us."

Giving

Through the practice of Radical Hospitality, we receive God and invite God's love into our lives. By practicing Passionate Worship we love God in return; God shapes our hearts and minds as we begin to see the world through God's eyes. We cooperate with the Holy Spirit in our own spiritual growth as we practice Intentional Faith Development. God calls us to make a difference in the lives of others, and we practice Risk-Taking Mission and Service. And at some point in our following of Christ, we realize all that we are comes from God and belongs to God; this leads us to the practice of Extravagant Generosity.

Hundreds of scriptural stories, parables, and verses focus on possessions, wealth, poverty, giving, gifts, offerings, tithes, charity, sacrifice, generosity, and sharing with those in need, providing a strong theological basis for giving.

In the Old Testament, people of faith practiced *first fruits*, the giving of the first and best of the harvest, livestock, or income for the purposes of God. Abram offered up a *tithe*, or tenth, of everything, and Jacob returned one-tenth of everything to God (Genesis 14:20; 28:22). The Psalms and Proverbs repeatedly encourage the sharing of gifts with God and with the poor. The prophet Malachi implores people to rely completely upon God, teaching them that when they practice the tithe they will find God's providence and promise to be true (Malachi 3:8-10). Giving reveals and fosters trust in God.

Jesus teaches that the widow who dropped two coins in the Temple treasury gave more than all the wealthier people because she, out of her poverty, gave all that she had (Luke 21:1-4). And he highlights the foolishness of the farmer who built bigger barns to contain his earthly possessions while neglecting those things that would make him rich toward God (Luke 12:16-21). With his story about Lazarus suffering at the front gate of the rich person's house, Jesus reveals God's disfavor with the wealthy who refuse to help those in need when they have the capacity to do so (Luke 16:19-31). How we use money matters to God.

"Giving, not getting, is the way. Generosity begets generosity" (Luke 6:38, *The Message*). Giving opens our souls to God's lead.

"For God so loved that world that he gave his only Son" (John 3:16). The root of generosity is God's love.

Paul says, "Have you ever come on anything quite like this extravagant generosity of God, this deep, deep wisdom? It's way over our heads. . . . Everything comes from him; Everything happens through him; Everything ends up in him" (Romans 11:33-36, *The Message*).

Paul writes, "You are familiar with the generosity of our Master, Jesus Christ. Rich as he was, he gave it all away for us—in one stroke he became poor and we became rich" (2 Corinthians 8:9, *The Message*). And Paul describes how the Christians at Macedonia gave not only according to their means but beyond their means, and then he pushes others to excel in their giving in the same way (2 Corinthians 8:3-6).

Where God's Spirit is present, people give.

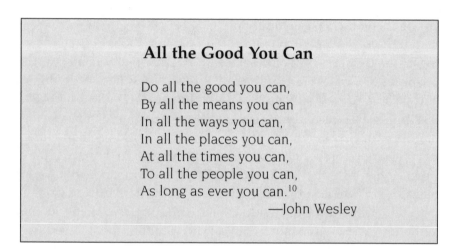

All the Good You Can

Do all the good you can,
By all the means you can
In all the ways you can,
In all the places you can,
At all the times you can,
To all the people you can,
As long as ever you can.[10]

—John Wesley

John Wesley wrote extensively on the use of money, the danger of riches, and the importance of giving. For Wesley, all things belong to God. This changes how we perceive the manner by which we *earn* money and *save* money, causing us to do so in appropriate ways. And it changes how we *spend* money, making us more responsible, and shapes how we *give* money. Wesley valued industrious and productive work, but he believed that acquiring money does not provide a profound enough life purpose to sustain the human spirit. When he wrote, "Earn all you can, save all you can, and give all you can," he drew an unbreakable link between acquisition and generosity, inviting us to use our material wealth to deepen our relationship with God and to increase our positive impact for God's purposes.

No stories from Scripture tell of people living the God-related spiritual life while fostering a greedy, self-centered, self-serving attitude. Knowing God leads to generosity.

Why Does It Matter?

Even with consistent teachings, many people wonder: Why become more generous? What difference does it make? How does something so material and mundane have anything to do with our spiritual lives? How does generosity help us flourish?

Giving Helps Congregations Thrive

Many people give simply because they love their church and they want the life-changing ministries of their congregation to prosper. They are themselves the beneficiaries of the church's ministries and they do their share to pay for the bills, the salaries, the facilities, and the costs so that the church can offer outreach, children's ministries, worship, and mission. They support the church so that others can receive what they have received. Their giving is functional and purposeful, a transaction that helps the church fulfill its mission and continue into the future. The fruit of this giving is tangible and visible; it is both immediate and long-term. Churches with generous members offer more ministry, work with greater confidence, have less conflict, and make a greater impact on their communities and on the world. Responsibility and hope for the church motivate the giver. People want their congregations to thrive.

Giving Aligns Us With God's Purposes

People give because their contribution aligns with the purposes God wants them to fulfill in the world. Helping people, relieving suffering, teaching the spiritual life, reaching young people—when we sense God's call to make a difference, we can contribute our time or become personally involved in the day-to-day ministry. Another way to make a difference is through giving, contributing the resources that make possible the work that we feel called to support. We please God by making the difference God wants us to make.

Why Wouldn't You Do It?

Paul and Carolyn have been leaders in their congregation for years, and their generosity has grown steadily as they have matured in faith. They also have enjoyed substantial financial success. When their church felt called to reach more people and younger generations by building a new sanctuary, Paul and Carolyn were challenged to give a major gift. They prayed about it for weeks, before deciding to give the largest gift they had ever given in their lives. "I felt like I was asked to partner with God for a great purpose," Paul said. "Our gift became one of the great delights of our lives. We loved knowing that we could make a difference. We were deeply moved by the experience." Carolyn adds, "If God gives you the capacity and the passion to do something, why in God's name wouldn't you do it?"

Giving Changes Us Inside

People give because generosity helps them achieve God's purposes in *themselves*. By giving, we develop the inner qualities of generosity. Generosity is not a spiritual attribute someone acquires apart from the practice of giving. It becomes discernable only through visible behavior. We cannot become generous and cling to everything we have without letting go. The opposite of generosity is greediness, selfishness, self-centeredness, and self-absorption. These are not the qualities that lead to life, and so by our giving we cultivate a different nature inside ourselves.

God uses our practice of giving to reconfigure our interior life. By giving, we craft a different inner desire as the driving element of life. Our motivations change.

Giving moderates the powerful and sometimes destructively insatiable drive for acquisition. In the daily interior struggle fostered by a consumerist, materialist society that pressures us to pursue many things that do not lead to real happiness, the practice of giving aims us at what ultimately satisfies. Giving sanctifies and deepens the struggle, and constantly resets the internal compass in the right direction. Generosity becomes a tool God uses to draw us closer to God and to align us more closely with God's desire for us.

Giving Mirrors God's Nature

We give because we are made in the image of God, whose essential nature is giving. We are created with God's nature imprinted on our souls; we are hard-wired to be social, compassionate, connected, loving, and generous. God's extravagant generosity is part of our essential nature as well. But we are anxious and fearful, influenced by a culture that makes us believe we never have enough. And we are scarred by habits that draw us away from God and that turn us inward with a corrosive self-interest. God sent Jesus Christ to bring us back to ourselves, and back to God. As we "have in us the mind that was in Christ Jesus," we become free.

Giving Fosters a Healthier Relationship to Money

Giving puts us in a healthier relationship with our possessions, and with the material world in which we live. We like making money, but we enjoy other things as well, such as the love of our family; belonging to community; a sense of meaning, accomplishment, contribution, and service. We enjoy making a positive difference in the lives of other people. But how do we maintain balance and perspective? How can we appropriately secure the basic needs of food, shelter, education, and health while also living with purpose? How do we avoid too much preoccupation with the things that do not ultimately satisfy, and cultivate those things that do? The intentional practice of generosity helps us keep our priorities straight.

When asked how much money they would need to earn to be happy, people of all different incomes answer the same. If they could only earn about twenty percent more than they presently do, they would finally arrive at a satisfying happiness. Persons earning $10,000 dream of reaching $12,000; those earning $100,000 believe that with just $20,000 more per year they will be happy; and people earning $500,000 believe that when they earn $100,000 more they will finally arrive. We pursue a receding goal. This is a prescription for never-ending unhappiness. We can never possess enough to satiate the appetite for more. Single-minded pursuit of lifestyles highlighted by pop culture keeps us stuck on the surface of existence, captured in the material world, unhappy with what we possess, and blind to the real riches.

When we accept unreflectively the myths of money, we suffer from a self-created, culturally-fostered discontent. Forty-year-olds feel like failures because they are not millionaires; families buy houses beyond their capacity to afford; people pine for what they cannot possess. We wallow in abundance while suffering from a self-proclaimed scarcity. Despite the fact that we live in better houses, earn more money, drive nicer cars, spend more on entertainment, and enjoy greater conveniences than ninety percent of the world's population, or than we ourselves enjoyed thirty years ago, we never have enough.

Tolstoy, in "How Much Land Does a Man Need?" writes about a man, Pakhom, who farms the land given to him by his father. He wants more, so he saves and sacrifices until he expands his acreage, and even this is not enough. He hears about another region where more land can be bought with less money, so he sells his farm and moves his family across the country to the larger spread. Still, he is dissatisfied. Finally, he hears about a place where the king is offering an extraordinary deal. If you give the king all your money, you may take possession of all the land you can personally encompass by walking around it in a single day. Pakhom imagines how far he could walk in a day, and all the land he could own. He sells all his property, travels to the new country, and pays the king in exchange for his chance to walk the perimeters of the land that will be his.

A stake is hammered into the ground before sunrise. Pakhom must return to the stake before sunset, and all the land that he circles before that time will be his. As the day dawns, he sets out. He runs at full speed in order to cover as much territory as possible. As the day heats up, he slows down and begins to circle back, but he sees lush pastures that he must possess, so he extends his path to include them. Late in the afternoon, he sees a stream that he cannot resist and so he enlarges his reach so this will be his. As the sun moves lower, he realizes that he has miscalculated, and he fears that he may not return to his starting place in time. He runs harder to reach the stake before sunset, pushing himself beyond exhaustion.

He comes within view of his destination with only minutes to go. Pushing dangerously beyond his body's capacity to continue, he collapses and dies within reach of the stake.

How much land does a man need? Tolstoy ends his short story by saying that "six feet from head to heel" was all he needed.[11]

We are surrounded by inducements that make us acutely and painfully aware of what we lack, more so than of what we have. Without beliefs and intentional practices that counterbalance the influences of culture, we feel discontent no matter how much we have. Extravagant giving is a means of putting God first, a method for declaring to God and to ourselves the rightful order of priorities. When we practice it, we live with a more relaxed posture about money, less panicked and reactive. We take possession instead of being possessed. Money becomes a servant rather than our master. By provoking us to give, God is not trying to take something from us; God is seeking to give something to us.

Every time we spend money, we make a statement about what we value. All inducements to spend money (advertising, social expectation, seeking to impress people) are attempts to shape our values. When we fail to conscientiously decide what we value and align our spending habits accordingly, a thousand other inducements and voices stand ready to define our values instead. Giving provides a spiritually healthy detachment from the most harmful influences of a materialist society, an emotional distance that is otherwise unattainable. Giving protects us from the pangs of greed.

Giving Encourages Intentionality

The practice of generosity opens us to deeper reflection and conversation about wealth and how it relates to purpose and happiness. Serious giving leads us to ask, What is our family's definition of success? How wealthy do we hope we, or our children, will be, and why? What motivates us as a household, and what matters most to our happiness? What will become of the wealth we accumulate? How much do we give, and why? What difference do we want to make in the world? How does giving influence our relationship with God? What does Extravagant Generosity mean for us? For God? These and other questions can only be asked with authenticity when they are supported by the practice of giving. Giving fosters intentionality.

Giving assists us in our quest for God. We cannot "pay" our way to a closer relationship with God; whether giving aids us in our relationship with God or not depends upon our inner attitude. However, an unrestrained appetite for wealth or clinging too tightly to what we possess can hold us back and cause us paralysis in our following of Christ. Scripture reminds us that "the love of money is a root of all kinds of evil" (1 Timothy 6:10), and "it is easier for a camel to go through the eye of a needle than for a rich man to enter the kingdom of God" (Mark 10:25, NIV). The rich young ruler cannot relinquish his wealth and so he forfeits life with Christ (Luke 18:18-25), the farmer builds bigger barns to store his possessions while avoiding eternal priorities and he loses his soul (12:16-21), the wealthy person ignores the sufferings of Lazarus at his doorstep and finds himself separated from God (16:19-31), the servant buries his talents instead of using them for his master and receives condemnation (19:12-26), and Ananias and Sapphira perish for their deceit that was motivated by their desire to keep their money (Acts 5:1-10).

Our clinging and coveting and hungering for wealth can obstruct our pathway to God and to the life God would have us enjoy. When unrestrained desire for material riches occupies the soul, there is little room left for God. Like Paul's assistant, Demas, we fall too much "in love with this present world," and we abandon Jesus' mission (2 Timothy 4:10). Greed impedes growth in Christ.

On the other hand, by giving generously, our beliefs and trust in God rise to tangible form. We become doers of the word and not hearers only. Giving makes following God real. We can live a God-related life or we can live without attention to God's presence and will. The God-related life means our relationship with God influences all we do. When we seek to do the things God would have us do, including giving, our practice intensifies our love for the things God loves. Then the material possessions that can serve as a distraction or impediment to following Christ become an instrument for our serving Christ. They provide an opening, a way of following, a vocation. Finite things open our hearts to spiritual callings, and created things deepen our relationship with the Creator. God's Spirit helps us become less attached to temporal possessions, and through the practice of giving, the same material things that might have tripped us up and turned us inward are used by the Spirit to carry us forward and to draw us outward. Our material goods, consecrated to God, nourish our desire to serve God. Generosity feeds our love for God.

Giving Honors Christ's Sacrifice

Finally, people practice generosity to honor the sacrifice of Jesus Christ. By giving extravagantly, we participate in the ultimate self-giving nature we perceive in the life, death, and resurrection of Christ. Transformation involves dying partially to the things we love. God gives us life. Our return gift is the giving of our whole selves to God. We give because we have received.

Ownership

The critical issue of ownership undergirds our theology of giving and stewardship. To whom do the material goods and wealth we enjoy ultimately belong? I'm not talking about the legal right of ownership, but rather a faith perspective—stewardship—that's rooted in thousands of years of Judeo-Christian theology and practice.

Fundamentally, we either consider the material things in our life—our money, house, property—as owned by God and belonging to God, and we manage them for God's purposes, or we view them as owned by us. If they are owned by God, then our tithes and offerings represent our returning to God what belongs to God already. What we keep also belongs to God, and we feel obligated to spend it wisely and not frivolously, and to invest it in ways that do not dishonor God's purposes. We try not to waste money or to live more lavishly than we should. We spend responsibly, allowing our relationship with God to form our minds. We manage God's resources as faithfully as we can.

But if we believe that our material resources fundamentally belong to us and that we entirely possess them ourselves, then we can do whatever we please with what we own, and our tithes and offerings are giving something that belongs to us, to God. God should be grateful for our generosity in giving a percentage for God's purposes rather than our feeling grateful for the privilege of using what belongs to God.

Which of these two views do we hold? Which perception is truest? Do the things of this life come from us, belong to us, and end with us?

For example, think about the possession of land. Suppose we hold legal title and own land according to civil authorities. In the larger span of the earth's history, does our patch of soil actually belong to us, or are we temporary stewards? The land didn't begin with us and doesn't end with us. The land we claim to own has existed for millions of years, was used by humans for millennia before us, and will remain for eons more after we are gone. For the ordering of civil life, we rightly say we own the property and it belongs to us. But our mortality assures that we are only the temporary stewards, managers, and keepers. At our dying, what will the things we own mean to us? Whose will they be? People live and perish, but purposes are eternal. With that understanding comes a profound and humble sense of responsibility about how we use the land. It's temporarily ours to enjoy, but we do so with respect and awe, because ultimately everything belongs to God, and not to us.

This concrete example applies to all of the temporal elements of our lives—our possessions, our wealth, even our bodies and minds. Which perspective is truer, more ethically sound, more aligned with reality? That it all belongs to us and we can do whatever we want? Or that we are the temporary beneficiaries, and we find meaning in using what God has entrusted to us to the highest purposes? Which perspective fosters better decisions and deepens a spiritually grounded sense of community and responsibility? The wisdom revealed in Scripture and tradition for more than three thousand years is that those who practice from the perspective of a steward find greater happiness.

Contentment

Generosity derives from a profound reorientation in our thinking about how we find contentment in life. Paul writes, "I have learned to be content with whatever I have" (Philippians 4:11). Paul was not a slacker, lacking in initiative! He was industrious, competitive, and ambitious for the work of God. Paul also realized how seductive our activity and our appetite for more could become. We begin to believe that happiness depends upon outward circumstance, visible achievements, and material comforts rather than deriving from inner spiritual qualities—love, peace, compassion, self-control, gentleness, prayerfulness.

Even possessing greater wealth and finer houses than most of the world does not mean that we experience contentedness. We can still feel panic, emptiness, striving, and isolation. When we base our self-worth on our salary, or on which neighborhood we live in, or what type of car we drive, then we race for more "meaning" by having more possessions. We feel needy, and our appetites become insatiable. Surrounded by water, we are dying of thirst. Feelings of scarcity paralyze us.

Breaking the cycle of conditioned discontent requires courageous soul work. It takes knowledge, insight, and the support of others to handle this from deep inside. The inner life shapes how we feel, what we value, and our attitude toward possessions. Contentment arises from seeking that which satisfies.

What Happens to God's Love?

"If you see some brother or sister in need and have the means to do something about it but turn a cold shoulder and do nothing, what happens to God's love? It disappears. . . . My dear children, let's not just talk about love; let's practice real love. This is the only way we'll know we're living truly, living in God's reality." (1 John 3:17-19, *The Message*)

Abundant living derives from generative relationships, from mutual support, and from knowing how to love and be loved. Flourishing results from a sense of purpose, of connection, of hope, of contribution. Contentedness comes from personal integrity, a life aligned with high values, depth of spirit and of mind, growth in grace and peace. These grant release from agitation, from unhealthy striving, and from continual dissatisfaction. Founded on these, we may value many of the things our culture induces us to seek, but without the harmful, destructive intensity. We want to improve our conditions and standing, but we don't embrace these objectives with the panicked intensity our society would have us do.

Primarily, contentedness is formed in us by the practice of generosity. Contentedness is learning to be happy with what we have rather than feeling distressed by what we lack. In our voluntarily giving away part of our wealth and earnings, we are saying, "I can spend all of this on myself, but I choose not to." In that simple act, repeated and deepened with frequency and intentionality, we break the bonds of self-destructive acquisitiveness. We can do it; we are free to choose! Contentedness comes with living beyond selfishness and egotism.

Second, contentedness results from a deep, cultivated sense of gratitude. Generous people are thankful. They perceive the gift-like quality in everyday tasks and ordinary friendships, and in common experiences and little treasures. They realize that the best things in life come gift-like, unearned, from beyond themselves, and are not created by them, but received by them. They give thanks in all things, and their gratefulness sharpens their awareness of the deeper sources of happiness. Their treasures are real and close and permanent, and unassailable by changes in the stock market. They give thanks for family, friendship, food, breath, the dawn of a new day, and for life itself. All is grace upon grace.

And contentedness results from the spiritual awareness that God has already provided us everything we need to flourish. We have enough; our income and home are sufficient. With sufficiency comes release from worry. Living more simply (and spending *below* our means rather than *beyond* our means) provides a countercultural path to greater peace. Sufficiency causes us to focus on what we *have* rather than upon what we *lack*. It keeps us from living in homes we cannot afford, driving cars whose payments overstress us, and taking jobs that disrupt our families and undermine other values we hold. Asking questions of sufficiency makes us clearer about what we really *need* in contrast to what we want or what our culture *says we need*. Living more simply and reflectively and intentionally, we thrive.

Finally, contentedness comes from persistent interior work and cooperation with the Holy Spirit to develop the personal habits that keep us from surrendering our sense of well-being, identity, and purpose to materialist measures. We are not always accurate at forecasting what will make us happy, or what will provide us increased well-being rather than a temporary boost. Living fruit- fully is not merely a matter of having something *to live on*, but something *to live for*. Purpose, connection, love, service, friendship, family, generosity—these sustain contentedness.

The Tithe

For hundreds of generations, the practice of tithing has sustained growth in personal generosity. To tithe means to give a tenth, and involves returning to God ten percent of income. It's simple, con- cise, and consistent. Write down your income for the month, move the decimal point over one place, and write a check to the church for the amount you see. Do it first thing when you are paid, and you discover that the practice dials down appetites, reshapes pri- orities, and that all other expenses, needs, and savings will re- adjust. What could be easier?

I heard someone say that the first time he wrote a tithe check, it felt like he'd swallowed an avocado pit! For most people, tithing is not easy. It takes time to learn and adapt and grow into the prac- tice.

Some people perceive the tithe to be nothing more than a left- over from an Old Testament law-based theology. They believe it is an arbitrary, technical rule with little relevance for later periods.

And yet Jesus commended the practice, even among the Pharisees whom he criticized for making a show of their self- righteousness. The early church practiced the tithe, and so have Christians in every generation since. John Wesley tithed and expected early Methodists to give regularly and generously at every class meeting and chapel service. Their gifts were meticu- lously recorded so that people could hold themselves accountable to the practice of giving.

The people whom we admire and respect for their generous spirits, spiritual wisdom, and deep-heartedness invariably have practiced giving in such an extravagant manner that it has reshaped them. God has used their long-term patterns of giving to form in them the spiritual qualities that cause them to be our men- tors. They give extravagantly according to their means, and many beyond their means, and most practice or exceed the tithe. The tithe remains a basic expectation of discipleship.

Name one person you admire and respect because of all they *keep* for themselves. Name someone you consider generous and spiritually mature who never gives, or who constantly complains about giving, or who always seeks to give the least amount required. Largeness of spirit leads to an eagerness to give our utmost and highest.

Tithing provides a consistent and universal baseline, a theologically and biblically faithful standard, that is nominal enough to allow people of nearly any income to meet without imposing great hardship and yet large enough to stretch us and to cause us to do the necessary reordering of our priorities that spiritually reconfigures our values.

Tithing provides a concrete way for us to take the words we speak, "God is Lord of my life," and put them into practice. Our commitment becomes tangible; our giving becomes a way of putting God first, an outward sign of an inner spiritual alignment.

Muscle Memory

Sarah grew up in a family that practiced tithing, and as a child she put ten cents in the offering plate from each dollar she received. She remembers receiving her first paycheck of $56 from her first job as a teenager, and her sense of achievement and delight when she gave $5.60 to the church. Now in her forties, Sarah has a high-paying job as a senior executive, and tithing continues to feel natural, a regular pattern of her life. She does it with ease and grace. "I love giving," she says, "and I cannot imagine living my life or loving God without giving back. Giving is one of the great joys of my life. Tithing was learned and practiced so early that I developed the muscle memory for giving. Like practicing my tennis serve for so many years that I don't have to think about each step, my giving is part of who I am." For someone beginning to tithe, Sarah's level of discipleship may appear unachievable. But with practice, anyone can develop "muscle memory."

Tithing challenges us to ask ourselves, Is my giving generous? Or merely expedient? Do I give for practical reasons to help the church, or for spiritual reasons to nourish my spirit?

Tithing is not merely about what God wants us to do, but about the kind of person God wants us to become. Does the giving I now practice help me develop a Christ-like heart?

Tithing requires honest prayer. What would God have me do? Are there things God would want me to give up in order to tithe? Many people have tithed even in the face of adversity, and have felt blessed doing so. The practice causes us to adapt our behaviors to someone else's will: God's. Tithing is not merely a financial decision; it is a life choice that rearranges all the furniture of our interior lives. That's why we do it.

One hundred and fifty years ago, our great-grandparents tithed if they were active people of faith. Why did they find it possible to tithe back then when we have trouble tithing today? Was it because they were so much wealthier than we are today? Absolutely not. The opposite is true. We have trouble tithing today because we live in more affluent times, and we have allowed our affluence to shape us more than our faith.

If you are new to faith and the prospect of giving ten percent appears overwhelming, take time to grow into the practice over a few years. Give proportionately—a set percentage of income, such as one or two or five—until you mature to the tithe. If you are facing unusual hardship, overwhelming debt, the loss of employment, or some other adversity, give as you are able during this season. But as stability returns, move toward the tithe in small incremental steps. With practice, tithing becomes easier, more natural. It will change your life.

On the other hand, if you have been an active follower of Christ and a member of a congregation for twenty, thirty, forty, or more years, and you have discovered the grace and love of God, participated in worship, matured through Bible study, and offered yourself in mission, and all these have provided for you a sustaining faith, but you do not tithe, then prayerfully consider why this particular spiritual practice does not apply to you? Why have you avoided this practice while embracing all the others? What makes this practice the exception? What makes you the exception?

Why Not?

Why do we sometimes find it difficult to give generously?

First, fear stops us from giving generously. We fear we may have to give up things that give us pleasure. And yet, plenty of people live happily and fruitfully who earn ten percent less than we do. Once basic needs are provided for, there is no correlation between income and happiness. But there is a strong relationship between giving and joy. Greed lessens joy; generosity increases it. That's as true as gravity. Ironically, fear and greed are what we most need to moderate in order to live happily, and the practice of generosity is the most potent antidote.

Second, people underestimate the spiritual work and practical planning required in order to take giving seriously. They innocently think that if they attend church, study the Bible, sing in the choir, and volunteer on service projects, that they will somehow absorb automatically a more profound commitment to generous giving. This is not true. Extravagant Generosity requires focused work, deep conviction, a mature spirit, learning, practice, and extraordinary intentionality. No one tithes accidentally. No one incidentally happens to leave an estate that rebuilds a congregation. Extravagant giving does not just happen.

Third, people convince themselves that they will tithe when they finally get a financial break that frees them to be generous, such as a large bonus, a promotion, a windfall inheritance, or winning the lottery. In fact, people tend to become less generous as they become wealthier. People who cannot find the spiritual courage to give from a lesser income are unlikely to find it easier to contribute from a greater income.

Fourth, some people feel called personally to give generously, but they do not receive support in their commitment from other family members. Don't you wonder what Zacchaeus' wife had to say when he arrived home and shared with her what he had said to Jesus that day (Luke 19)? Was she angry, bitter, resentful? Or had she been longing for the day when Zacchaeus would come to his senses and return to his best self?

Finally, some people feel that money and wealth are simply not appropriate topics for spiritual reflection and teaching. They divide their spiritual lives from what they do with financial matters. And yet Jesus frequently addressed wealth as a matter of faith. Greed, charity, saving, inheritance, riches, treasure, giving, wealth, poverty, taxes, sharing—these are all topics of faithful exploration. Jesus embeds our faith in the gritty details of hard decisions made daily at work and home.

Despite the outward challenges, the inner struggles, and the countercultural nature of generosity, where there is a desire to give, there is a way. The two coins dropped in the treasury from the hands of the poor widow, noticed by Jesus and recorded for all time as a model of Extravagant Generosity, forever reminds us that there is always a way.

The Practice of Extravagant Generosity

The practice of Extravagant Generosity stretches us to offer our utmost and highest to God rather than to give in a manner that is haphazard, unplanned, reactive, minimalist, mediocre, or mechanical. People who practice Extravagant Generosity give with unexpected liberality; they make giving a first priority; and they plan their giving with great energy and passion. They go the second mile. They do not give from a "what remains" mentality, but from a "what comes first" priority. Giving seriously becomes a personal spiritual discipline, a way of serving God, and a means of helping the church fulfill its God-appointed mission. Focused conviction and intention causes them to give in a more pronounced way, without fear and with greater trust. Giving changes their lives.

Extravagant does not correspond with giving that is merely dutiful, required, burdensome, mandated, or simply doing one's part. *Extravagant* denotes a style and attitude of giving that is unexpectedly joyous, without predetermined limits, from the heart, extraordinary, over-the-top, and propelled by great passion. *Extravagant* is the generosity seen in those who appreciate the beauty of giving, the awe and joy of making a difference for the purposes of Christ. Extravagant Generosity is giving to God as God has given to us.

People who practice Extravagant Generosity change their lives in order to become more generous. They shift things around so that they can do more. Their generosity opens them to projects they never dreamed God would involve them in! They become rich in giving.

They support ministries marked by fruitfulness and excellence, and they expect accountability and transparency. They are conscientious and intentional. Generosity is their calling. They want their giving to make a difference. They care.

They grow in the grace of giving. They learn. They take small steps until tithing becomes natural. They deepen their understanding of giving through prayer and Scripture, and they foster generosity in others. They give more now than in the past, and will give more in the future than they do today.

They push their congregations to become more generous, focusing more of their resources beyond their walls through mission and service. They advocate outward-focused ministry.

People who practice Extravagant Generosity do not wait to be asked. When they see a need, they step forward to meet it, offering their resources as a means of help. They never expect to be catered to or begged by other church leaders to do their share. They do not give to control the church but to support it. They excel in giving. They love to give.

They give extravagantly with conviction. They are motivated by a desire to make a difference rather than by guilt, fear, desire for recognition, or to manipulate others. They give with humility.

And yet, they are willing to serve as an example to motivate others, to teach and lead and bear witness to the power of giving. They draw others toward generosity, and toward God.

They teach their children and grandchildren to give, mentoring them by example on how to earn honestly, save carefully, spend prudently, and give lavishly.

They not only give out of present income, but occasionally they give from investments for major projects. When appropriate, they leave a portion of their estate for the church through their will. Their giving outlives them.

They look at difficult financial times through the eyes of faith rather than of fear. They persist in doing good. They give in all seasons.

They view personal success as a reason to share.

They enjoy giving. They pray and hope and dream about the good they accomplish through their gifts. They consecrate their giving to God. They delight in generosity.

They accept appreciation graciously when it comes, but they do not pine for acknowledgement or thanks. They give expecting nothing in return.

People who practice Extravagant Generosity learn to enjoy things without possessing them, to moderate their acquisitiveness, and to find satisfaction in simpler things. They avoid personal debt as much as possible. They save. They avoid overindulgence, ostentation, and waste. Their possessions do not rule them. They aspire, like Paul, to know the secret of being content with what they have.

They live with a sense of gratitude. They give thanks in all circumstances. Love is a gift, and life is grace.

They give generously beyond their church, contributing to causes that strengthen community, relieve suffering, prevent diseases, and make for a better future. They change lives. Their giving knows no bounds.

They delight in receiving money, find pleasure in its responsible use, and experience joy in giving it to God's purposes. They do not become too attached, and are not stopped, deceived, slowed, misled, or detoured in their following Christ by the possession of money. They are rich toward God.

As If For the Very First Time

Charles Frazier, in his novel of the American Civil War, *Cold Mountain*, introduces a minor character, a fiddler whose life is changed through an incident that causes him to look at his musical talents in a whole new way.

The fiddler is a drunk, who plays only for drink, and he knows only six songs. His military unit camps near a house where there's a powerful explosion. A young girl is severely burned in the explosion and is near death, and her father sends for a fiddler to help ease her way to heaven. The fiddler doesn't know what to do; he's afraid, and enters the dark cabin where the young girl suffers in excruciating pain. From her deathbed, she says, "Play me something." He plays a tune. "Play me another." The fiddler plays his drinking tunes slowly, thinking it more appropriate to the circumstances. Soon he has exhausted his small repertoire. "Play me another," she says as she struggles against the pain. "Don't know no more," he says. "That's pitiful," she says, "what kind of a fiddler are you? Make me up a tune then." He marvels at such a strange request. It had never entered his mind to try such a thing. But he has a go at it. Soon the girl passes away. Her father thanks the fiddler for lifting her to heaven with his fiddle.

A transformation takes place, and the author writes, "Time and time again during the walk back to camp he stopped and looked at his fiddle as if for the very first time. He had never before thought of trying to improve his playing, but now it seemed worthwhile to go at every tune. . . ."[12] Thereafter, he never tired of trying to improve his playing, and he went into taverns of every kind to study the sounds and methods of other musicians. He learned more than 900 tunes, and composed many of them himself. "From that day . . . on, music came more and more into his mind. . . . His playing was as easy as a man drawing breath, yet with utter conviction in its centrality to a life worth claiming."[13]

Picture him looking at his fiddle as if for the very first time, realizing that he can change lives with it and that he can lift souls to heaven. Imagine the difference he made in the lives of people and the meaning that was added to his own life. That ordinary fiddle and the simple gift of music, when used for higher purposes, became sacred. When he discovered the gift he had been given, and the power of that gift to influence the world for good, he was changed.

Before his incident with the girl, it had never occurred to him to want to improve, but now with new purpose, he couldn't get enough of his gift of music. His ordinary talent became beautiful, a source of joy and meaning.

We find something similar through the practice of Extravagant Generosity. Giving causes life. Before, our giving may have been arbitrary, perfunctory, haphazard, a little here and there. But when we discover the great difference generosity makes; place it in service to God; and use our resources to relieve suffering, strengthen communities, and restore relationships, then we look at giving entirely differently. We look at our giving, and see it as if for the very first time. We discover that something as ordinary as our giving can help lift souls to heaven and change lives for the purposes of Christ. We want to improve on our generosity at every turn until it becomes as easy as drawing breath.

Through our generosity, God can do extraordinary things. Through our giving, God changes lives, and in changing them, transforms us.

Questions for Reflection

• Who first taught you to give? Who modeled generosity for you? How are you continuing to learn to give?

• What motivates you to give? How does giving shape your relationship to God? How does your giving to God influence other aspects of your life?

• When was a time you felt God's Spirit move you to give your resources beyond what you had previously practiced?

• What's the largest gift you have ever given in your life? What motivated you? What resulted from the gift, and how did it affect you?

• How do you feel about the statement "all things belong to God"?

• How do you feel about tithing? Do you practice proportional giving or tithing? If so, why? If not, why not?

• What obstacles prevent you from giving extravagantly?

• When was a time you felt God transformed your life because you gave?

CHAPTER SIX

Fruitful Living and Offering God's Love

*"Be ready to speak up and tell anyone who asks why you're
living the way you are, and always with the utmost courtesy."*
—1 Peter 3:15, The Message

Vines, branches, seeds, vineyards, farmers, fig trees, harvests, sowers, soils, weeds, roots. *Fruitfulness* provides a metaphor for many profound aspects of the spiritual life and the Christian journey.

In the Old Testament, fruitfulness refers to future generations, to progeny, and the promise of an abundance of heirs to God's covenant. Imperative and promise intertwine. "Be fruitful and multiply" (Genesis 1:28).

Jesus uses fruitfulness to draw our attention to the impact, the consequence of our life in Christ. He describes kingdom fruit, the effect and promise of the reign of God and the difference it makes to live in God. Fruit refers to what Christ accomplishes through us. Jesus cursed the fig tree that bore no fruit and describes the pruning of fruitless branches. Fruitless means inconsequential, ineffectual, showing no result. As with his message with the parable of the talents, Jesus' expects our life of faith to make a difference.

Jesus says, "My Father is glorified by this, that you bear much fruit and become my disciples" (John 15:8). Fruit evidences discipleship; following Jesus and fruitfulness are inextricably linked. Disciples bear fruit.

Jesus sends disciples "to every town and place where he himself intended to go" (Luke 10:1), and asks for their help with the harvest, referring to the desired result of changed lives and transformed conditions that he hopes the disciples will reap. In the parable of the sower, some seeds fall upon stony paths and among choking weeds. Nevertheless, seed finds fertile soil and a harvest comes forth. Jesus was reminding his disciples not to feel discouraged, to keep at it, to remain faithful to the task. Seeds grow unseen. Fruit is unrevealed until its season.

"The kingdom of heaven is like a mustard seed," Jesus teaches (Matthew 13:31). The smallest of seeds leads to the greatest of trees. This passage encourages patience. Unanticipated and consequential transformation emerges from the most surprising sources.

Paul uses similar metaphors to explore inner growth, the fruit of the Spirit—love, joy, peace, patience, kindness, generosity, faithfulness, gentleness, self-control (Galatians 5:22-23). Fruitful living cultivates these essential qualities of soul and character. Fruitfulness refers to the interior growth and the reconfiguration of the soul that becomes visible in outward changes of attitude, behavior, and value. Followers grow in grace.

In all cases, fruitfulness refers to what results from what we've received, the change wrought within us and through us by the Holy Spirit, and the impact we have with our lives. The quality of effect God has on our inner lives and the resulting outward impact we have on the lives of people around us—these comprise spiritual fruitfulness.

When Jesus says, "I am the vine; you are the branches," he reminds us that all our fruit derive from our relationship to God in Christ. Our fruit is God's fruit.

The word *fruit* refers to the way plants reproduce. Fruit contain seeds that multiply and create life apart from the original plant and yet related to it. Through fruit, life passes along to another generation. Fruit is new life. Fruit is growth. Fruit is future.

Radical Hospitality. Passionate Worship. Intentional Faith Development. Risk-Taking Mission and Service. Extravagant Generosity.

These are the practices of fruitful living. By repeating and deepening these, we cultivate interior fruit of the Spirit as well as grow in our capacity to serve the world for God's purposes. All are interwoven in practice, with each fostering inner growth and each manifesting outward consequence. However, *receiving God, loving God in return, and growing in grace* especially feed inner fruitfulness, while *serving others* and *giving generously* particularly bear fruit in the world around us. Fruitful living changes us inside, and through us transforms the world for God's purposes.

The Reason God Has Mingled You With Others

"It is the nature of the divine savour [salt] which is in you, to spread to whatsoever you touch; to diffuse itself, on every side, to all those among whom you are. This is the great reason why the providence of God has so mingled you together with [others], that whatever grace you have received of God may through you be communicated to others . . ."[14]

—John Wesley

Offering God's love to another person and inviting someone else to follow Jesus multiplies both the inner qualities of spiritual fruitfulness and the outward impact of service more than anything else we could possibly do. Living fruitfully includes passing along the faith and creating spiritual life in others. Fruitful living involves inviting others to the spiritual life.

Offering God's love so that others may accept God's grace bears fruit beyond what we can fathom. Imagine if as a consequence of your following Christ and your invitation, a few other people explore the spiritual life who otherwise might not have done so. Imagine if these people eventually embrace following Jesus themselves, mature in faith, and make a difference in the world through their service, mission, and giving. Imagine how the people you invite to faith intermingle with the lives of countless other people you do not know. The fruit in your life multiplies in unseen and unknowable ways when we offer God's love. The grace of God is replicated, repeated, and shared. Seeds are scattered, some take root and bear fruit in ways beyond what we can comprehend.

When I think back to those who opened the door to the spiritual life for me and invited me in, many people come to mind. Youth directors, pastors, lay volunteers, and friends welcomed me and made me feel like I belonged. They taught me, corrected me, laughed with me, worked alongside of me, and formed in me a yearning for God. They offered God's love and helped me open my life to that love. They pulled me along. Mostly they listened and shared and prayed and served. They were a means of grace, a manifestation of God's searching and initiating love. Their methods took ordinary forms—youth ministries, retreats, campfire music, hiking trips, service projects. Interspersed with these activities were a thousand special moments, personal conversations, poignant insights, shared experiences, private encouragements. The combined effect of their efforts was a persistent and intentional offering of God's love. They demonstrated the acceptance of me by God that I accepted, the love that changed my life. Their seed-casting found fertile soil. Their persistence made ready the soil. Many of the people who first offered me God's love are now deceased, and others I've lost touch with. Most remain forever unaware of their influence on me, and yet every life I touch becomes an extension of their ministry, the fruit of their life in Christ.

Offering God's love multiplies the fruitful life. By offering Christ, we complete God's grace, the grace we received when we invited God into our lives and made room for him in our hearts. The receptivity that opened our hearts to God opens doors to others. Our lives become a doorway through which people enter into the spiritual life. God with us becomes God through us. As we invite and encourage others into the life of Christ and stimulate their spiritual exploration, we perceive God working through us. We become "ambassadors for Christ, since God is making his appeal through us" (2 Corinthians 5:20). Grace becomes tangible through invitation.

Mark and Diana

Mark and Diana never imagined becoming part of a congregation. Mark grew up in a family of inactive church members. He only remembered occasionally attending Christmas services as a child. Diana had no church background, and her perceptions were formed by caricatures of pastors and church people from television. She felt indifferent toward religion, somewhat suspicious about the motives of church people. Diana and Mark married in their early twenties, and a year later they had a baby daughter.

Doorway People

Many Christians can name one or two people who were critical to their entry into the faith community. Perhaps a pastor, a relative, a neighbor, or a coworker offered the first invitation, provided encouragement, or welcomed them. Even in larger congregations, an unusually high proportion of newcomers have been influenced by a small handful of people. These "doorway people" have a natural way of gently helping people along on the critical first steps toward faith. Who are the "doorway people" for your own faith journey? For whom are you a doorway person?

Mark worked as an assistant manager at an auto parts franchise before finally landing a job in financial services, the subject of his college preparation.

With a baby in the family, they looked for a new place to live. They met Tom, who managed apartments and rental properties. Also in his twenties, Tom was amiable and helpful. He seemed genuinely interested in their well-being. They came to know him better as they visited homes with him. Tom asked them if they were part of a church. His question was casual as he gathered information to find them a home in the right place. They said they were not church people. Tom simply stated that he and his wife, Debbie, really enjoyed belonging to their congregation. He left it at that.

Their friendship with Tom continued to develop, even though they never rented any of his properties. Tom and Debbie went to dinner with them several times, and Tom invited Mark to go fishing with him. From time to time, Tom would weave some experience at their church into the conversation, commenting about an upcoming project or activity for the children. Tom and Debbie never pushed, but Mark and Diana could tell that faith involvement was important for them. Months after first meeting them, Tom and Debbie offered their first specific invitation to a church event when they told Mark and Diana about the church softball team, and invited them to practice.

The invitation sounds simple and innocent, but it led to considerable conversation between Mark and Diana. Diana remembers wondering what a church team would be like. Would they pray? Because they felt safe with Tom and Debbie, they agreed to play, and they enjoyed the team, feeling at home among the other young adult couples and singles. They received reminders in the mail of the weekly practices and games, and they looked forward to the time together. They had not realized how isolated they had felt as a couple focused on raising a young child, and their time with others their age refreshed them.

Late in the season, the team was invited to a dinner at the home of one of the members. They met other young adults from the church there, including the pastor and his wife. Looking back, Diana tells how that party had been a huge step. The time together felt natural, with lively good-humored conversation. The pastor began with prayer, and invited people to introduce themselves. He handed out announcements about a new Bible study that would meet twice a month in homes with child care provided at the church. Tom and Debbie would host the study, and he encouraged people to sign up. For reasons neither of them can describe, Mark and Diana looked at each other and nodded, and that night they signed up for the house group. The Bible study became a steppingstone toward more involvement.

As Mark and Diana describe their journey into faith, they highlight a crucial turning point for them, the tragic death of a baby who was a child of a couple from the softball team. As grief swept through the young adult group, they wanted to help their new friends—offering to pick up relatives from the airport and helping with the meal after the funeral. They were moved by the genuine support shown by the entire church. "That's the moment it clicked for me," Diana says. "I wanted to be part of a community like that. We needed that in our lives." Diana and Mark met with the pastor, and joined the church the following Sunday. While all their beliefs about God were far from settled, they clearly belonged to a loving community.

The events described above took place more than twenty-five years ago. Mark and Diana are now in their mid-fifties. They continued to get more involved in the church and in deepening their faith. Worship became a natural pattern of their life. They have attended dozens of short- and long-term Bible studies over the years, and they have also taught them. They served a stint as youth sponsors when their own children were in junior high. They have repaired roofs in Honduras, built wheelchair ramps in Mexico, and delivered meals to shut-ins. They have sat at the bedside of their friends in the hospital and prayed for them. They've developed a rich personal prayer life.

The Most Likely Pathway

"Do you, as the way opens, share Christ with people who do not know Christ? Do you witness to your faith by letting your life speak?" These questions, adapted from a Quaker covenant, remind us of the gentleness, simplicity, and persistence that underlies effective invitation. Many people with no church home are respectful, curious, and open to spirituality in general. Others are hostile, resentful, or suspicious of religion, perceiving church people to be offensive and hurtful.

Even people who are not particularly open to church are nevertheless open to their friends, and to the experiences that their friends value. The most concrete and personal way God reaches out to invite people into faith is through friends who invite friends.

Most people who have no church have at least one friend who practices the faith, and that person provides the most likely pathway to the spiritual journey. Are you that person?

"It's uncanny now to think about the significance of Tom's invitation to us. We discovered later that Tom constantly invited people into the congregation and nudged them along in their Christian walk. I can't imagine what our lives would be like without the faith community. The church has given us our closest friendships. Following Christ has changed everything about us—how we rear our children, how we treat each other, how we see the world. It's been an amazing journey."

The meaning of an event is determined by what follows from it. A simple inquiry about church affiliation or an ordinary invitation to join a softball team can fall into complete meaninglessness among thousands of conversations that we experience regularly. On the other hand, Tom's simple invitation changed two lives forever, and through them also transformed the lives of their children. Those simple gestures of invitation and initiative became the door to new life, the entryway to a relationship with God. Those invitations were God's initiating love. They were pathways to Christ.

An essential element of our life with Christ involves our finding the courage and the voice to invite others to Christ.

Come and See

As we deepen the practices of fruitful living, our friends see us grow. They sense the trajectory of our life. They see us maturing in Christ as our beliefs take visible expression. Faith becomes real to them as it becomes real for us. Our life becomes a catalyst for others, and we give them courage to try it, to take the first steps, to explore the interior life and the community of Christ.

Tom offered simple descriptions of something that mattered to him. His language was natural, personal, and yet unapologetically invitational. He did not insist or argue nor even speak explicitly of faith. He let others look over his shoulder to see what he was doing.

The Gospel of John opens with profound philosophical expressions: the eternal Word becomes flesh and dwells among us, the Light shines into the darkness, and "from his fullness we have all received, grace upon grace" (John 1:16). The high theological rhetoric moves quickly down to earth with specific stories about people. By the end of the first chapter, Jesus forms disciples, and then disciples invite other followers one after another, all of them repeating a simple refrain, "Come and see." Invitation begins the gospel. This is John's way to emphasize the essential quality of offering God's love. "Here's what I have found. Come and see."

Invitation

Invitation represents one of the most persistent themes in the teachings of Jesus.

Jesus forms his disciples with the words, "Follow me." He initiated conversations with the woman at the well, visited with farmers in the fields, engaged tax collectors, entered homes, approached sickbeds, and consoled mourners. He had an out-ward focus, looking to the margins of the crowd to draw people toward God. He did not wait for people to discover him or to find the courage to move his way. He moved toward them.

Jesus' most compelling parables portray the initiative of God, a love that searches and seeks and waits and persists and refuses to give up on anyone. The lost sheep, the woman and her coin, the father and his son, the Samaritan and the stranger—all describe an active love that steps toward people. If we want to do what Jesus does, we search, seek, and serve.

Critical actions reveal whether Jesus' followers have embraced the kingdom. "I was a stranger and you welcomed me . . . I was in prison and you visited me" (Matthew 25:35-36). These express an active outward focus. And following Jesus involves being sent to invite others, with this advice: "Don't load yourselves up with equipment. . . . you are the equipment" (Luke 9:3, *The Message*).

Key words remind us of our "sentness." *Apostle* comes from the Greek *apostolos*, and means "someone sent out." The word *mission* derives from Latin, and means "to send off." We've been assigned a task, entrusted with a duty, given a calling. As *disciples* (meaning *learners, followers* of a person or idea), we do the things Jesus did and teach what Jesus taught. Our *mission* is to communicate the love of God, to offer God's grace. Every follower of Christ becomes part of the mission and is sent out as "ambassadors of Christ." We carry out our mission in our own context. We've been assigned a duty and provided a setting, such as our workplace, neighborhood, and family network to seek those who need God's love. Followers invite people who do not know Christ to know Christ.

Why do followers of Jesus feel compelled to tell others about God's love?

God's love has an initiating quality that searches and seeks and never gives up on anyone. Grace is the gift-like, reaching-out love of God. God's love is active, assertive, penetrating, embracing. It spills over, flows outward, and seeps into every corner of human life. God's love pursues. This love propels Jesus' followers to the ends of the earth.

John Wesley, the eighteenth-century founder of Methodism, felt compelled to reach the underclass workers and miners who could not find spiritual sustenance in the Anglican church of the day. He broke the rules and acted against his own natural inclinations and training. In his own words, he "submitted to be more vile" when he moved out of sanctioned church buildings and began to preach in the early mornings on roadsides and in fields to reach people otherwise unreached by the gospel. Wesley cringes as he talks about the breach of clergy etiquette that led him to such an audacious and assertive move. He was willing to go places he didn't want to go and do things he didn't want to do in order to align with the outward thrust and searching nature of God's grace. He felt the initiating quality of God's grace required him to do so. Methodists were driven by the desire to offer Christ.

Can there be any doubt from Scripture or from our founding ancestors about the imperative of inviting? Some find it difficult to do what Tom and Debbie did, to invite acquaintances into the community of faith. Yet, such simple words can change a person's life forever.

The most mysterious element of the decline of mainline churches is our unwillingness to invite others in a gentle, authentic, and natural way. It's as if we believe that what we have experienced in our own faith journey is of no value. Somewhere the movement characterized by "go to" instincts settled into a "come to" church, and the deliberate, searching, seeking, sharing, outward-focused quality of discipleship quieted into a restrained passivity that waits for people to find us. We have developed an attitude that says, "Let those who know nothing of God's love come to their senses and show up at our place on Sunday morning." We can do better.

The initiating and invitational posture is essential to discipleship. Invitation completes us—there are depths of the inner life that remain beyond our experience without offering Christ. The receptivity that opens us to God leads us to encourage, welcome, and support others. Invitation continues God's love. In us, the Word becomes flesh once more.

Why the Ambivalence?

If following Christ involves inviting others to explore the inner life and to discover the riches of God's grace, why do we feel so ambivalent about this?

First, we perceive matters of faith and spirit to be so private and personal that for us to speak openly and invitationally feels intrusive. We fear offending people, as if by telling a friend about our serving or the worship we love, we appear judgmental toward them since they do not do these things. We gladly talk about which bank we use and which doctor we visit. But talking about our delight in working with children at church or the sense of community we find in singing with the choir—these are less comfortable topics. We cordon off experiences of worship, service, or prayer from the ordinary sharing of daily life. We avoid the spiritual life.

Belonging, Behavior, Belief

An emergent church advocate describes a generational change in how people connect to faith communities. In the past, entry into the religious life proceeded from belief to behavior to belonging. People would profess what they believed in order to join, and then they would behave like the community (worship, service, etc.), and finally they would experience belonging as they were accepted by others. Now, she says, a person's journey into faith communities moves from belonging to behavior to belief. People first must experience acceptance and support. Then they practice the behaviors of the community, such as serving the poor, praying, and worshipping. Finally, after months of belonging and practice, the new person realizes, "Gee, I really do believe this stuff about God. I never thought I'd hear myself say that." Creating a sense of belonging is the entryway to belief.

Second, in a live-and-let-live world, we feel uncomfortable with any notion that we may be imposing our values onto others. To propose universal truth claims from a particular vantage point today sounds arrogant and close-minded. We feel an inexplicable unease with the notion that we have something others need or know something others don't. Self-righteousness offends us.

Third, the thought of praying, preparing, and planning to invite another person into the faith community feels manipulative, artificial, contrived, and utilitarian. Intentionality connotes conniving. The invitation benefits the "inviter" more than the "invitee" as the genuine hospitality of Christ dissolves into a membership drive, a marketing ploy, a surface activity not unlike recruiting people to join a club. When the success-equals-growth culture pushes the process, the invitation lacks sensitivity or respect for the inner life. We see it as *our* invitation rather than *God's*. We despise self-serving motives.

Fourth, invitation reminds us of negative stereotypes of evangelism done rudely—the street corner preacher screaming invectives at passers-by, or the pushy college roommate constantly shoving religion our way. The last person any of us wants to sit beside on an airplane is the stranger wanting to save our soul! We chafe at attempts by people to squeeze us into their mold through pressure, insistence, or guilt. They overstep appropriate interpersonal boundaries when we feel cornered and coerced, and we want nothing to do with practices that cause others to feel that way about us. We reject pushiness.

Fifth, we find it difficult to offer the invitation in a healthy manner that fits our theology and temperament because we don't have many good examples to learn from. Ironically, each of us has come to faith or remained on the journey because of the encouragement of other people, and evidently their disposition toward us was not off-putting, offensive, or coercive. In fact, we give God thanks for the gift of their witness! And yet, we hesitate to do for others what has been done for us. We lack models.

What personal qualities attracted us to them? What stimulated our curiosity? What practices supported our inner yearnings and helped us to experience God's grace, and to eventually say *Yes* to God?

A Deep-Rooted Love

For me, the inclination to invite others comes from a deep-rooted place inside. It is grounded in the grace I have experienced, an initiating love that sought and found me, and that brought me God's unconditional love. This deep-rooted desire to share God's grace is something God-given and sacred, a calling. It is as tangible as my personal call to follow Christ.

From the depths of my soul, I desire for people to love and to be loved, to experience a sense of purpose from serving others, and to believe that their life matters. I want people to feel connected, immersed in community, surrounded and sustained through all the setbacks and celebrations of living. I genuinely desire for them to discover the inner life, and to learn to ease the suffering of greed and the pain of empty strivings. I want them to discover that love is the better way, that patterns of violence and manipulation can be interrupted, that loneliness can be overcome and suffering relieved, and that there is a depth to life that is sacred and holy and worthy of exploration.

The spiritual life changes us and moves us from agitated to stillness, from anger to peace, from distressed about our own situations to compassionate about the circumstances of others. I want people to discover life with God.

I want people to flourish, and for people to feel that life is worth living and people are worth loving and God is worth trusting. I don't try to force anyone into a mold. I don't want others to make all the choices I've made. But I want them not to be alone, and to know that God loves them and that the things that matter most—love, hope, peace, purpose—are attainable when we open our hearts to God and follow the way we see in Jesus. In Christ, a well-known road takes us to unknown places of enchantment, mystery, and meaning.

In my own way, always and everywhere for as long as I live, I want to say, "Come and see. Come and explore grace, kindness, peace, humility, and hope. See what it's like to make a difference and to let Christ interweave our lives into the fabric of community. Come and see."

Offer God's love. Invite. Pray about it. Learn about it. Grace received becomes grace given; a way discovered becomes a path offered. Our awakening awakens others. The clever, nervy, impossible love that pushes open a door in our souls glimmers through us enough to be seen by others.

Grace becomes real through invitation. What's the greatest gift you have ever given? Perhaps the most life-changing gift you will ever offer to another person is an invitation to life with God. This is the gift immeasurable. Come and see.

As the Way Opens

The church fulfills its mission at the margins of the congregation, where those who actively follow Christ encounter those who are not a part of the community of faith. Picture a congregation as concentric circles of relationship, with those who know each other well and offer leadership in the middle, those who faithfully volunteer a little farther out, and those who are newer or less active a little farther still. When we reach the edge of the farthest circle we discover on the other side the people who are not a part of a community of faith. The church fulfills its mission at that edge, through *service*—helping, serving, or relieving suffering; and through *evangelism*—inviting, welcoming, and sharing faith. In a healthy church, the boundary is wonderfully permeable, and members readily reach across the edge and new people easily enter into the community. That margin is where the action is. That's where the church fulfills its mission. The mission of the church is not fulfilled in church planning meetings comprised of church members talking with other members, although such meetings may be important. *Hearers* and *talkers* become *doers* at the margin.

If the frontline of our work, where church people encounter non-church people, is at the margins, then how do I, as a bishop, do my part to fulfill the mission of the church? I'm surrounded by district superintendents and conference staff, who are themselves surrounded by pastors, who are surrounded by lay leaders, who are surrounded by congregational members. I can live, breathe, and work in a world totally insulated from the mission of church. I could spend the rest of my life speaking to no one but United Methodists! I could fill every day with appointments with pastors, meetings with congregational leaders, chairing task forces, serving on committees, and attending events for women's organizations and men's ministries. Everyone would applaud and support me for the attention I give them. Yet, I would have no idea what's happening at the margins where the church fulfills its purpose, and I would lose sight of the mission of the church. Pastors face the same risk, and so do the active lay leadership in congregations. How do we break the pattern of self-contained, inward-directed ministry?

As a leader of the church, if I don't fulfill the critical invitational task of Christian discipleship, then I cannot with authenticity and integrity ask others to fulfill a mission I'm unable or unwilling to do myself. This parallels the issue of tithing. The unwillingness of a pastor or lay leader to tithe stifles the entire congregation's capacity to grow in generosity. When the pastor and lay leaders do not tithe, then their pleadings for others to do so sound inauthentic and hollow. People intuitively know when leaders are unwilling to do what they are asking followers to do—the small hesitations, the sideways glances, the awkward laughter betray a certain spiritual discomfort. Similarly, if pastors and congregational leaders do not learn to offer invitations to faith, then they sound inauthentic and empty when they ask others to do so. Their unwillingness to personally invite others stifles the invitational capacity for the whole congregation.

As a bishop, I've had to think about where I personally encounter people who have no faith community. For me, it's in my travel—in airports, restaurants, shuttles, hotels, convenience stores, and car rentals. That's where God has placed me at this point in my life. It's my small part of the larger mission field of the church.

Some months ago a young man in his twenties was helping me at a car rental agency. He took my credit card, and as he typed computer keys he asked me about employment. I told him that I work for The United Methodist Church.

He looked up and said, "Really? I went to a Methodist church when I was a kid." I asked him where he grew up, and which church he had belonged to. He seemed pleasantly open to talking about this, and so I asked if he remembered who the pastor was back then, and he gave me the name and spoke with fondness about his memories of the pastor. I told him where the pastor was living in retirement. The conversation was comfortable, mutual, and nonintrusive, so I proceeded a step further, and said, "I'm curious to know if you still belong to a congregation." He and his fiancée had lived in the area for three years, and they sometimes talk about visiting a church, but they never have. She is from another denomination and her family never attended church. I suggested that if he and his fiancée ever decided to visit a church, they might be pleasantly surprised by what they would find at some of them, and I mentioned the names of two churches. He looked up from the computer, handed me a pad of paper, and asked if I would please write down the names of those churches. He seemed genuinely appreciative.

As I prepared to leave, another employee stepped out from the back office, a man in his forties. He saw me and said, "You're the bishop!" He had heard me preach at his congregation some months before, and he began to tell me about his many church involvements—how long he had been a member, committees he chaired, mission teams he had worked with. He loved his church and was a faithful member. He had worked at the rental agency for more than a decade.

Have you figured out the point of this story yet?

These two people had worked together for three years. God had placed these two people together and had entrusted one of his disciples with the task of invitation. In three years of working together, the seasoned disciple had never taken five minutes to have a gentle conversation that might restart a faith journey for someone waiting and wanting that to happen.

How do we find our voice, our manner, our way to reach out to others? We don't have to stand on the street corner and scream about Jesus like a crazy person, or go door-to-door pestering strangers and intruding into their homes, or change our theology. We only need to practice our theology and become an instrument of God's grace! Find your approach and prayerfully discern when the time is right to offer a gentle invitation. Look around where you work and where you live, where you eat and where you shop. Offer a gentle invitation that may change someone's life forever.

Imagine if you had one such conversation a month. Imagine if one quarter of your congregation's membership had one such conversation each month. It would change your congregation. It could change the lives of people in your community. It would change you.

While sitting in an airport lounge that had become crowded because of flight delays caused by a storm, I overheard bits of conversations around me. Two business women in their twenties were sitting near me with their laptops, file folders, and briefcases. They talked about business while intermittently trying to contact spouses about the flight schedules. As the weather intensified, more flights were delayed, and people attempted to rearrange personal plans.

One of the women became increasingly concerned by her failed attempts to reach the person she was trying to call. She shared with her colleague that she had planned to get home in time to make one hundred sandwiches to take to a soup kitchen, and she needed to reach the program director to let her know she was delayed. The sandwiches are given out with hot soup for homeless families at a shelter. She does this twice a month with her church.

Her friend asked her why she was so worried. "Won't it be OK to miss this one time?"

"I made a commitment, and I've got to hold up my part or find someone else to take my place. Besides," she said, "we just can't know what it's like to be hungry, to be really hungry and vulnerable and not know where the next meal is coming from. They're depending on me."

There was a long pause. Then the second woman said, "If you ever need help with that, let me know."

The first woman's face lit up, "That would be so cool. You'll be amazed. It's a whole different world. I'd love showing you how it works."

Conversion is an intimidating term weighted down with so much baggage that sometimes we overlook how small and incidental a first step toward faith might appear. What happened between these two colleagues was a slight turning toward God, the new opening of heart and mind toward serving others, which is an essential quality of the spiritual journey. Personal witness, simply expressed, stimulates first steps.

The woman above offered a simple description of something that matters to her. Her language was natural, personal, and yet unapologetically invitational. She let someone look over her shoulder to see what she is working on. Her practice of openness to God extends into a ready receptivity toward others, a posture of hospitality and encouragement.

Do I expect that the the rental car employee or the woman at the airport will show up for the 11 o'clock service next Sunday, join the choir, sign up for a Bible study, and start tithing? No, not at all. I don't know what the next few years will bring in their lives, and I can't foretell all the ups and downs they will face. But I pray that their curiosity about the spiritual life will deepen enough to take a next step, and that through the positive invitation offered by me or

others, they will find a faith community that helps them grow in
the life of grace.

Christ Evident in Each One

In the early years of Coca-Cola, the soft drink company
decided to develop a distinctive bottle that would stand out
from all other drinks. They thought about shape and color and
label and logo. One instruction for the design was, "Even if the
bottle shatters into a million pieces, we want each piece to be
identifiable and recognizable as being from a Coke bottle."
What they designed met that criteria, and in the days of glass
soft drink bottles, if you ever saw the light green pieces of
glass on pavement, you knew the kind of bottle they were
from.

How do we live so that our life speaks a clear witness that
we are part of Christ, even when we are away from the church?
Some congregations develop such a rich sense of community,
identity, and witness, that even when you meet individual
members far away from the church, their distinctive depth of
commitment and compassion shines through. Christ is not
only evident in the community, but in each member of the
community in beautiful ways.

If everyone in your congregation—pastor, staff, musicians, lay
leadership, volunteers, members—offered the same quality and
frequency of invitation that you do, would your congregation be
growing or dying? A significant element of our decline is the
personal unwillingness of individual disciples to comfortably and
consistently invite others into the community of faith and into the
life of Christ. When we pray for renewal for our congregations, we
can't ask God to do for us what God created us to do for God. If the
people reading this book don't find their voices and offer invitation, then nobody else in the church is likely to do so either.

Invitation is our mission. Offering God's love is our work. God
wants us to succeed at this even more than we want our church to
be renewed.

Bearing Witness in All Things

What is it about your life or mine that would make someone else want to be a follower of Jesus Christ, a person of faith, a part of a congregation?

The purpose of inviting other people to follow Jesus is to help them rediscover love—God's love—and to provide a community that gives sustained focus, energy, and resources to developing the spiritual life. No other community besides the church has as its purpose the deepening of such elements of the human soul as hope, forgiveness, generosity, service, joy, peace, justice, gentleness. Love is the key to unlocking the door to ultimate reality, and in the community of Christ we intentionally practice receiving God's love, loving God in return, and loving others. We invite people into a life of love, surround them with the everlasting arms of God, and encourage them to do the same for others. We love because God first loved us.

To bear witness to Christ involves more than inviting people with words. It means living with such grace and integrity that our lives themselves become appealing to others. The second chapter of Acts reports that people were drawn into the way of life of the followers of Christ. They found Christian practice utterly compelling and irresistibly appealing.

Is this true for us? We are inviting people to reconfigure their interior lives. That's an audacious request. They must see in us qualities that make them think, "I want what you have." People are hungry for something that is going to make a difference, and they want to be part of something that matters. Do they see in us "the mind that was in Christ"?

By Reason, Truth, and Love

"Never dream of forcing [other people] into the ways of God. Think yourself, and let think. . . . Even those who are farthest out of the way never compel to come in by any other means than reason, truth, and love."[15]

—John Wesley

Some months ago, I was eating in a family diner in a small town. The place was crowded, and I sat by myself in a corner booth. Four older adults sat at the table in the center of the room. They spoke in voices that made them easy to overhear, and all of us in the restaurant got an earful! They began to talk about their pastor in excoriating terms, and then moved on to the pastor's wife, the irresponsibility of the finance committee, the vote of the trustees, the budget, the grounds committee. They were grim, intense, hostile, and animated by anger. They stoked one another on. It was ugly and embarrassing, and I watched other people in the restaurant trying to avoid them. After nearly thirty minutes of this, they paid their bills and stepped out into the parking lot where it appeared that their conversation continued. When the waitress brought my tab, she rolled her eyes and told me that they come in two or three times a week and do nothing but complain about their church.

What about the content or tone of that conversation would make anyone want to follow Christ? Why would anyone want to get within six blocks of that church? As followers of Christ, every word we speak bears witness to what following Christ means.

The people we admire and respect and who have loved us into the faith are not perfect and neither are we. Followers of Christ sometimes overcome things; other times they feel stuck and small and alone. They struggle. They don't vanquish every adversity, and they doubt and hurt and question. They are persons of faith set on a journey toward Christ whose way they can't always clearly see.

But through intentional practice, they move forward; the community pulls them along and connections get them unstuck. They tap interior resources that give them strength. They set their lives upon a foundation. They live with resilience. They face disappointment and loss just like everyone else, but they cultivate threads of connection to God and other people that pull them through. God uses their disciplined intentionality to change them.

Are we living the kind of life that would make others want to live like us?

Witness is more than verbal invitation. It is a way of life that invites God to work through us.

Offering God's Love

Those who offer Christ realize that the journey begins with a per-sonal relationship, leads to a comfortable invitation to a ministry of the church, and results in an embracing of the spiritual life. They trust God's time. A visit to church represents a brush with the body of Christ. They invite.

People who invite others train themselves to feel comfortable talking about spirituality and the interior life with outsiders by sharing about God with other members of the faith community. They practice until speaking of faith feels natural.

They share their faith struggles as well as their trust in matters of spirit. They don't pretend to know what they don't know. They speak with humility.

They pray about particular people who have no faith commu-nity. They prepare themselves for when the moment is ripe for gen-uine, honest, simple, and nonthreatening invitation. They ask God's guidance to notice when the way opens.

Encouraging new people toward Christ enriches their own spir-itual life. They humbly accept the gift of serving as an ambassador of Christ. What people wear, how they speak, the subcultures they inhabit, and the lifestyles they choose—these things create no bar-rier to their practice of grace. A judgmental attitude closes people out and cuts off dialogue. They view people through God's eyes. They rule no one out.

They trust in God's time. Sometimes it takes decades before a person opens to the first conscious step toward Christ. They would rather go lightly than to adopt an intrusive attitude that is patron-izing, manipulative, or guilt-inspiring. They give people space.

People who consciously bear witness to Christ attend to small actions. They know the power of unexpected grace. They listen when no else seems to care, express sympathy when no else notices, and take time when everyone else rushes on. God uses simple expressions of grace to incrementally pry open the human heart.

They believe that the church is the body of Christ and a principal means of grace. Belonging to a congregation leads people to Christ.

Some specifically train in order to offer God's love in unusually hard circumstances, such as with victims of crime, those suffering

159

grief, recovering addicts, inmates, refugees, the homeless, and the mentally challenged. They go where they know Jesus would go.

Reaching others is not about membership numbers or the survival of the institution, but about connecting people to God. Their motive is Christ.

People who offer Christ realize that faith is a journey of a thousand incremental steps, and that everyone moves toward Christ from different places at different paces. Pathways to Christ are many.

They let Christ's invitational nature pervade all their work. They involve outsiders in the work of serving the poor and weave those they serve into the community of faith. They open doors.

Their approach is other-centered. They listen more than they speak. They let the Spirit lead. As the way opens, they invite.

They never force, coerce, insist, or misuse the name of God to instill fear or guilt as tools to pressure people. "Grace upon grace" is their means. God makes ready the human heart; they trust the prevenient grace of God.

Procrastination is disobedience in slow motion, and so they don't postpone, avoid, resist, or deny the importance of offering God's love.

Our experiencing grace and following Christ remain incomplete until the love of God flows through us into others. We know half the truth if we entirely understand grace according to what we receive, the love God has for us, the light shining into our lives. If grace gets in, but can't get out, then we diminish our capacity to grasp what God has entrusted to us.

Offering Christ completes us, and accomplishes God's purpose. Opening ourselves to God's grace involves opening the treasure for others, and inviting them in. Inviting God into our hearts leads to inviting others into the heart of God. Radical Hospitality toward God becomes Radical Hospitality toward others.

Questions for Reflection

- Who first offered God's love to you? Who invited you into the community of faith and made you feel welcome? What did they do to create a sense of belonging for you? How have you acknowledged their influence or expressed appreciation to them?

- When was a time you were aware of God moving toward you in some spiritual way? When was a time you felt God moving you toward another person?

- How have you invited someone to a ministry or service of the church? What made the time ripe for the invitation?

- When was a time you had a conversation about the spiritual life with someone who has no church home? How did that feel? How did the experience affect them? How did it affect you?

- What do you consider your obstacles to offering God's love to others? What makes invitation difficult for you?

- If you asked yourself the question, "Do I live a life that would make someone want to follow Christ and be involved in a faith community?" how would you answer?

Epilogue:
Changed From the Inside Out

Through the personal practice of *Radical Hospitality*, we open ourselves to God's unconditional love, and make room in our hearts for God's grace. We cultivate receptivity; we invite God in.

With patterns of *Passionate Worship*, we love God in return, allowing God to change our hearts, learning to love what God loves and to see the world through God's eyes.

Through the practice of *Intentional Faith Development*, we cooperate with the Holy Spirit in our own spiritual maturation and follow Christ more nearly.

We discern God calling us to make a difference in the lives of others through the practice of *Risk-Taking Mission and Service*.

Eventually, we realize that all that we have and all that we are belongs to God, and we practice *Extravagant Generosity*.

These Five Practices of Fruitful Living, as we repeat and deepen them, shape our perceptions, attentiveness, attitudes, and behaviors. They change us. We grow in grace and in the knowledge and love of God. And we cannot help but share what we have discovered, and we offer God's love to others.

The five are a *set* of practices—intertwined, interactive, and interdependent. Progress on one pulls us forward in another. Learning in one area supports growth in all areas. Exploring worship strengthens receptivity; practicing service makes generosity more desirable. Cultivating one practice makes another more approachable. They fit together and complement one another. Five discernable threads form one cloth, the fabric of faith.

The ordered listing may lead us to conceptualize the practices as sequential steps or as a linear progression, and yet growing in grace seldom happens so straightforwardly. John Wesley, as he teaches about prevenient grace, justifying grace, sanctifying grace, and the meaning of inner holiness and outward good works, presents these "in order of *thinking*" rather than "in order of *time*."[16] He's suggesting that this is the order we use to explain them clearly, but in real life they are more intertwined, less linear. Grace doesn't order itself logically; God's Spirit is free of the sequences we use to describe its presence.

The same is true with the Five Practices. In fruitful living, the order is pleasantly irregular and surprisingly unpredictable. Some people enter the journey with Christ through service; others through a growing sense of belonging. Some are "struck by grace" while working in a soup kitchen and others while singing with a praise band. An act of generosity may spark the receptivity that invites God in and leads us to open a Bible for the first time. Small steps in one area are followed by giant leaps in another; there is ebb and flow, growth and setback, detour and recalibration. These are the essential practices that move us along the path in following Christ; nevertheless, no two journeys look exactly the same. Fruitful living is "a garden with a thousand gates."[17]

Don't feel overwhelmed by the Five Practices. Fold them gradually into patterns of living. Take them in stride. Cultivate them. Accept a gentle sense of urgency about the direction, but patience about the progress. Following Christ is lifelong.

How do we have the mind in us that was in Christ Jesus? How do we cultivate a life that is abundant, fruitful, purposeful, and deep? How do we live a genuinely good life that pleases God, and makes a positive difference? Spiritual practice answers these questions.

Nothing sustains spiritual practice more than belonging to a congregation. Personal practices are learned, rehearsed, and supported in churches. Community worship supports personal prayer; joining a class stimulates spiritual growth. A congregation serves as a catalyst for fruitful living. And spiritually healthy leaders serve as a catalyst for the congregation becoming more effective in its mission. Fruitful congregations foster fruitful living, and vice versa.

The flourishing life results from repeating and deepening these practices, from the lifelong project of cooperating with the Holy Spirit. As we learn to listen for God and to invite God in and to work with God, our lives are shaped. We become new creations in Christ, and we arrive at places we never expected.

Changed From the Inside Out

"So here's what I want you to do, God helping you: Take your everyday, ordinary life—your sleeping, eating, going-to-work, and walking-around life—and place it before God as an offering. Embracing what God does for you is the best thing you can do for him. Don't become so well-adjusted to your culture that you fit in without even thinking. Instead, fix your attention on God. You'll be changed from the inside out." (Romans 12:1-2, *The Message*)

Everybody already worships something, whether we are conscious of it or not. Habits and practices already form us, purposefully or without conscious intent. Society cultivates appetites for exactly the things that do not ultimately satisfy. We unthinkingly adopt these values when we make no conscious choices; these are our gods unless we open ourselves to something deeper.

There is another way. God loves us and desires a relationship with us. Loving God in return changes us. Growing in grace deepens our experience of living. Serving others gives us something to live for. Living well involves keeping these truths in sharp awareness. The Five Practices take us to the things that last.

Through the Five Practices, we worship what is worthy. We choose what satisfies. We accept a deeper serenity. The practices focus us. They represent sustained obedience in a consistent direction, a daily honoring and serving God. They help us stay in love with God.

~~To find and follow Christ and to serve him—that is fruitful liv-~~ ing. These practices are a way forward, tested and true. They invite us along a pathway prepared by hundreds of generations that embeds us in community, connects us with God, and provides avenues for us to make a difference. They re-enchant the world for us. They tumble us headlong into the mystery of life. They show us a way.

When Jesus said, "I am the way, and the truth, and the life" (John 14:6), he was not speaking arrogantly, egotistically, or narrow-mindedly. He was expressing a genuine desire to turn us, to redirect us away from things that do not satisfy and toward the things that cause us to come alive. The time given to us on this earth is infinitesimally small compared to time itself, and so he desires for us to live it richly. Jesus asks us to build our houses upon solid rock rather than shifting sand. He invites us. He wants us to flourish.

To be a follower of Jesus is to take this path, to step by step grow into the life that really is life. God through Christ reveals the way, invites us along, and walks with us. Following Christ will change you; and through you, God will change the world.

Notes

CHAPTER 1

1 All Tillich quotes and references in this chapter are from his sermon, "You Are Accepted," contained in Paul Tillich's *The Shaking of the Foundations* (Charles Scribner's Sons, 1948); pp. 161–162.
2 Anne Lamott, *Traveling Mercies* (Anchor Books, 1999); p. 141.
3 John Wesley, *Works*, Vol. 1, "Journal From Oct. 14, 1735, to Feb. 1, 1737-8"; p. 103.
4 For further discussion of this paradox and the trends and sources of happiness, see Dick Meyer's book *Why We Hate Us: American Discontent in the New Millennium* (Three Rivers Press, 2009).
5 Joe Eszterhas, *Crossbearer* (St. Martin's Press, 2008); pp. 3–5.

CHAPTER 3

6 Wesley, Vol. 8, "A Plain Account of the People Called Methodists"; p. 260, paraphrased.
7 Wesley, Vol. 5, Sermon 24 "Sermon on the Mount"; p. 296.

CHAPTER 4

8 Frederick Buechner, *Wishful Thinking* (HarperSanFrancisco, 1993); p. 119.
9 *The United Methodist Hymnal* (The United Methodist Publishing House, 1989); p. 607.

CHAPTER 5

10 This quote is attributed to John Wesley.
11 Leo Tolstoy, *How Much Land Does a Man Need? and Other Stories* (Penguin, 1993); p. 110.
12 Charles Frazier, *Cold Mountain* (Atlantic Monthly Press, 1997); pp. 231–232.
13 Frazier; pp. 232, 234.

CHAPTER 6

14 Wesley, Vol. 5, Sermon 24 "Sermon on the Mount"; p. 299.
15 Wesley, Vol. 5, Sermon 37 "The Nature of Enthusiasm"; p. 478.

EPILOGUE

16 Wesley, Vol. 6, Sermon 45 "The New Birth"; pp. 65–66.
17 Carl Koch, *Garden of a Thousand Gates: Pathways to Prayer* (Saint Mary's Press, 1998).